"This book is a trustworthy interpretation of both Marxism and Christianity. It can be used in a number of church settings: parish-based lay education, seminary classrooms, continuing education courses, church libraries. The authors combine faithfulness to the gospel with fairness in dialogue with Marxism in its many forms."

CARL E. BRAATEN

"This book is very much needed in our American churches today because it corrects the tendency to think of Marxism as being monolithic and the tendency to be blinded by hostility toward any movement as soon as we see in it signs of Marxist influence. It is discriminating in discussing the relation between Christianity and Marxism and it has come out of deeply Christian concerns."

JOHN C. BENNETT

"A substantial study document. I know nowhere else in the modern literature of the subject where the thought of the great revolutionary is so concisely presented and so clearly evaluated in its strengths and weaknesses from the angle of Christian understanding."

CHARLES C. WEST

CHRISTIANS
& THE MANY FACES OF
MARXISM

CHRISTIANS

& THE MANY FACES OF

MARXISM

WAYNE STUMME, Editor

AUGSBURG Publishing House • Minneapolis

Library of Congress Cataloging in Publication Data

Main entry under title:

CHRISTIANS AND THE MANY FACES OF MARXISM.

  Cover title: Christians & the many faces of Marxism.
  Bibliography: p. 156
  1. Communism and Christianity—Addressses, essays, lectures.   I. Stumme, Wayne, 1929-   . II. Title: Christians & the many faces of Marxism.
HX536.C379 1984   261.2'1   84-10980
ISBN O-8066-2087-0 (pbk.)

Manufactured in the U.S.A.   APH 10-1195

1   2   3   4   5   6   7   8   9   0   1   2   3   4   5   6   7   8   9

Contents

Marx: The Man and His Thought

Historical Development of Marxism

Christian Encounter with Marxism

Contributors

DR. FAITH E. BURGESS
Academic Dean and Professor of Church History
The Lutheran Theological Seminary
Philadelphia, Pennsylvania

DR. JAMES M. CHILDS JR.
Dean of Academic Affairs and Professor of Ethics
Trinity Lutheran Seminary
Columbus, Ohio

DR. WILL L. HERZFELD
Pastor of Bethlehem Lutheran Church, Oakland, California
Vice President, The Association of Evangelical Lutheran Churches
Adjunct Professor, Pacific Lutheran Theological Seminary,
Berkeley, California

DR. PAUL T. JERSILD
Professor of Ethics
Wartburg Theological Seminary
Dubuque, Iowa

DR. MARC KOLDEN
Professor of Systematic Theology
Luther Northwestern Theological Seminary
St. Paul, Minnesota

DR. TIMOTHY F. LULL
Professor of Systematic Theology
The Lutheran Theological Seminary
Philadelphia, Pennsylvania

DR. PAUL V. MARTINSON
Professor of Missions
Luther Northwestern Theological Seminary
St. Paul, Minnesota

DR. RUSSELL B. NORRIS JR.
Pastor of Zion Lutheran Church
Hollidaysburg, Pennsylvania

DR. WAYNE C. STUMME
Assistant Director of the Division for
Theological Education and Ministry
The American Lutheran Church
Minneapolis, Minnesota

DR. RONALD F. THIEMANN
Chairperson and Professor
Department of Religion
Haverford College
Haverford, Pennsylvania

Foreword

by Paul A. Wee

This book addresses the origins and contemporary manifestations of one of the most pervasive and yet misunderstood of the world's ideologies, Marxism. It seeks to provide inquiring Christians with a clear, readable introduction to the person and thought of one of the most influential historical personalities, Karl Marx, and to the variety of world views and social-economic-political systems propagated in his name today. It is not intended, however, to be a defense of either Marx or any of the "many faces" of Marxism; rather it seeks to make a modest contribution to the cause of understanding by tapping one of the most powerful resources the church has to shatter the barriers of prejudice and fear—telling the truth in love.

The underlying question which this book seeks to address has been expressed with some urgency in recent years by member churches of the Lutheran World Federation (LWF) who suddenly found themselves face to face with the actual challenge of Marxism in one or another of its forms. The challenge is this: How does the Christian church, both theoretically and practically, deal realistically with radical (Marxist) movements for social change? While Christians in explicitly Marxist nations such as the Soviet Union, the German Democratic Republic, and the People's Republic of China were searching for new ways to express the meaning of the gospel, churches in other nations such as Chile, El Salvador, Guatemala, Nicaragua, Namibia, Ethiopia, and Rhodesia (now Zimbabwe) were finding themselves pulled relentlessly into the matrix of revolutionary change.

11

In Ethiopia, on the eve of the revolution which he favored but which finally turned against him, Gudina Tumsa, general secretary of the Ethiopian Evangelical Church Mekane Yesus, made an urgent request: "Please send us books dealing with Marxism and Christianity . . . we are not prepared for what is coming." In Namibia, following the slaughter of over 600 of his people by the South African Defense Force on Ascension Day, May 4, 1978, the late Bishop Leonard Auala, patriarch of the Evangelical Lutheran Ovambokavango Church, lamented, "In the face of this violence against our people we are given no choice but to seek help from those who follow Karl Marx." The same sentiments were expressed by Bishop Jonas Shiri, president of the Evangelical Lutheran Church in Zimbabwe, in a speech before the Lutheran World Ministries Commission in New York. While indicating gratitude for the churches' support for his people during the struggle to overthrow the white supremist government of Ian Smith, Shiri also noted the large debt of his people to the Marxist nations, especially to the People's Republic of China.

In response to the many-faceted challenge occasioned by these events the Lutheran World Federation responded by mobilizing the resources of its units and member churches. The Commission on World Service provided humanitarian assistance to people in revolutionary and post-revolutionary (nation-building) situations in Mozambique and Zimbabwe, for example, where Marxist governments welcomed the church's continued support to their people, and even provided literacy and agricultural training in Ethiopia where the new Marxist government carried on a vicious repression of the church. The Commission on Church Cooperation brought together church leaders and world mission units to reflect on the new situations in light of the church's mandate to proclaim the gospel in word as well as in deed. Among the more significant consultations carried out by the LWF's Commission on Studies were those dealing with "The Encounter of the Church with Marxism in Various Cultural Contexts," "Implications of the New China for the Christian Mission in the World," and "The Identity of the Church and its Service to the Whole Human Being" (Ecclesiology Study). While the effects of material assistance and the findings yielded by these study processes cannot be measured with accuracy, there is no question that they helped prepare a number of Lutheran communities to face a challenge for which they would otherwise have been ill-prepared.

At the same time it became increasingly clear that out of this complex web of involvements by Lutherans in movements of social change a sharply focused question was emerging. Yet it was a question which was not directed to churches in those nations of the Third World which were presently involved in struggles for social change within their boundaries, but to "churches in the North Atlantic Region" which, as one recommendation of the Ecclesiology Study observed, "participate in their countries' power structures which dominate the world." Similar recommendations urged these churches "to conscientize their people about their present involvement in American and European exploitation and domination." Speaking of the Western churches another recommendation asserted that "by pointing to the root causes of the worldwide inequalities and injustice in the world trade system, they can become a sector of critical public opinion." At its Sixth Assembly in Dar es Salaam, Tanzania in 1977, moreover, the LWF affirmed "the need for radical change in the world's economic system as one essential step toward attaining peace." The message was not antagonistic, but it was certainly clear: the Lutheran churches in North America should reexamine their own policies, as well as those of their governments, to determine if they help or hinder the realization of the dignity, freedom, well-being, and peace which the Lord intends for all people.

While not wanting to imply that Christians and Marxists could not live together in peace or that some manageable form of Christian-Marxist synthesis was not possible, the implication of this request was unavoidable: if Western institutions, including Christian churches, continue to participate in the exploitation of people and raw materials in Asia, Africa, and Latin America, the people of these countries will have no alternative but to turn for help to those who espouse some form of Marxist ideology. In fact some church leaders were drawing a more pointed general conclusion: Marxism will succeed in becoming a rallying cry of hope for the world's poor in direct proportion to the failure of the Christian church to take seriously the source of transforming power for individual and social life which belongs inherently to the gospel of Jesus Christ.

It was in response to this challenge that the Lutheran World Ministries Commission, on the recommendation of its Standing Committee on Studies, called a major consultation in 1983 on the theme, "The Challenge and Necessity of the Christian-Marxist Dialogue" and commissioned the writing of study material for the laity, pastors, congregational groups, and students to help them become better equipped to deal with the many types of Marxism and the challenges they pose to the church. The result is this book edited and written by Dr. Wayne Stumme and an exceptional team of scholars who hold a variety of views on the meaning of Marx and Marxism but who all stand firmly within the evangelical-catholic tradition of the Lutheran church. For the members of the Task Force on Marxism, the five-year process which has produced the consultation and this book has been an adventure in learning and self-discovery. It is their hope that this will be your experience also.

On behalf of Lutheran World Ministries, I want to express my gratitude to Dr. Stumme, the chairman and guiding spirit of the Marxism Task Force, and to his able team; to Dr. Eugene Brand, under whose guidance as Director of the Office on Studies this study process began; to my colleague Dr. David Burke who, as successor to Dr. Brand, continues to explore the creative implications of these studies for the life of the church, and to Ms. Davida Goldman, who has not only provided superb secretarial and administrative assistance, but has given of her deep commitment to the church to see these projects through. It is my personal hope that this book, written in a style well suited to the informed lay person in the congregation, will occasion a rethinking of some of the stereotyped images we have of Marx and Marxism as well as a reexamination of our mission as Christians to proclaim God's Word to the conditions and causes of poverty, hunger, injustice, and oppression which Karl Marx and many of his disciples sought to address.

PAUL A. WEE, GENERAL SECRETARY
LUTHERAN WORLD MINISTRIES

Introduction:
Why Study Marxism?

by Timothy F. Lull

The Locked Bookcase

When I was growing up in Fremont, Ohio in the 1950s, I spent a lot of time at the town library. As a teenager, I moved out of the "Youth" section and into exploring the resources of the adult section of the building. And I quickly noted that one cabinet with glass doors and curtains was always locked.

Once or twice I saw a librarian scurry up to that cabinet, take out a book, and hurry away with it to the circulation desk. And so I asked a friend who worked in the library what was so special that it had to be kept in a locked bookcase.

I should have known. He told me that it was not considered acceptable to have books on sex out on the regular shelves. So those things that the library owned along that line were kept under lock and key, but could be obtained by persons with the proper credentials. He also added that certain other kinds of books that were considered too controversial were kept in that safe place.

I wanted to know more. What could possibly rank with sex as a topic to keep hidden? "Well," he said, "I happen to know that they have books in there on China."

"China?" I asked, thinking that he meant plates and cups. "You know, Communist China," he explained. I knew they were our enemy and had been since the Korean War. But that still didn't explain to me the high anxiety about those books.

Now, 25 years later, I think I understand. I know that all books about communism and about Karl Marx had been, at that time, considered too controversial in a small town for general library circulation. Certain books were safe—J. Edgar Hoover's *The Enemy Within* or *What You Must Know about Communism*. But in the years after Senator Joseph McCarthy frightened America about the Red Menace, communism—and even Karl Marx—seemed too dangerous for study and discussion.

Many readers of this book will remember the period that I am discussing. Those of us who grew up before 1960 will remember how easy it seemed to summarize communism in a few words—menace, atheism, Stalin, labor camp, godless materialism, subversive. Those readers who were born later may find all of this confusing. And yet almost all of us in North America have felt that we knew as much about Marx or Marxism as we needed to. It is that assumption which this book wishes to challenge. We want to unlock the glass bookcase and permit all of us to take a closer look at Karl Marx and the many faces of Marxism.

The Shock of Complexity

This book is not an apology for Marx or Marxism. But it is an admission that the half-dozen words used in the past will not explain the complex phenomenon that we know in the world today as Marxism. In the years since 1960 we have been learning more about the diversity of Marxists around the world. Most people have come to see that Russia and China—for all their common features of government—are as much rivals for power as partners in a conspiracy for world domination.

So we have begun to learn that political movements which draw their inspiration from the writings over a century ago of Karl Marx (1818-1883) are very diverse and cannot be summarized in a simple way. There are socialist governments in Europe, socialist experiments in East Africa, Marxist and non-Marxist revolutionary movements in Central America, and states in the world like Cuba or Libya that claim to be socialist, Marxist, or communist in some sense.

Our *first hope* for the reader of this book is: *growth in knowledge of the diversity of governments, political parties, and revolutionary movements that claim to be Marxist*. This book does not offer a catalog of all such movements, but rather something of a history of their major types and ideas that they might have in common for all their diversity.

Some readers will reject the notion that there is any significant diversity or complexity in Marxism. For them the old slogans of international conspiracy and godless communism still explain adequately what they read. And it is clear that the recent tensions between the United States and the Soviet Union have perhaps given a new persuasiveness to the notion that all of this can be seen as a great worldwide struggle between good and evil forces.

That was not our finding in the study that led to the writing of this book. Marxism does have many faces. It is not a simple notion of world revolution by the workers, but a complex fabric of ideas and practical proposals. Some are more prominent in certain movements; others are dominant in others. And in every case the shape of Marxism in a given country is greatly influenced by the local history, traditions, and views of reality.

Marx and Marxism

Readers of this book will be familiar with the problem of understanding how one Jesus could be the founder of and influence so many different forms of Christianity. A similar problem exists with Marxism. It is difficult at first to see how diverse movements can all trace their origins back to a man who has been dead for 100 years.

But this leads to a *second hope* for readers of this book: *growth in knowledge about the life and thought of Karl Marx and of how the major forms of Marxism trace their inspiration back to him.* In many ways it is surprising that a scholar who spent most of his life writing books that are extremely difficult to read should have such an effect on the history of the world.

Yet Marx was a complex figure. He wrote a great deal. And like Luther, there are some tensions between his early writings and his later writings. Also like Luther, while he had great scholarly ability, he was also a first-rate communicator with ordinary, working people and was able in his more popular writings to respond to many of their complaints and aspirations.

This can be seen clearly in a reading of Marx's *Communist Manifesto* (1848) written with his colleague and lifelong coworker Friedrich Engels. Here one sees ideas reaching toward action; here the results of research into how history works lead beyond study to a revolutionary cry: "Workingmen of all countries, unite!" And even those who do not find hope in that cry will want to understand it better. The road to take toward that understanding is one that must include some strong consideration of the leading ideas that stem from Karl Marx himself.

Some will say that communism has so badly betrayed Marx's vision that one can learn very little about the world today from such a study.

And it is clear to us that the hopeful vision of Marx himself has to be measured against the terrible things that have happened in his name—whether in true or false loyalty to him, we cannot yet say. But this brings us to the debates within Marxism about how to follow his lead, about which features are permanent and which can be changed, about which ideas represent the heart of his legacy to the world.

Encounter with the Churches

Some readers will be surprised, even shocked, to find a church publisher involved with such a project as this. But it is precisely in encounters between Christians and Marxists in many parts of the world that new interest in Marxism has arisen. For many decades it seemed that Marx's critique of religion and practical atheism (of which you will read more in the coming chapters) made any dialogue with religious people impossible. One simply had to choose whether to be a Marxist or a Christian.

But that old dichotomy is challenged today. Many on the Christian side will now admit that much of Marx's critique of the churches of his day was correct and even courageous. Too many of the churches had become totally subservient to the wishes and interests of the ruling, wealthy classes. In too many places the industrial poor were neglected by the parishes. Marx, it would be argued, saw many things that Christians should have seen, but instead ignored.

And on the Marxist side—for whatever reasons—an admission emerges from some that religion may have been a more positive force in history than Marx sometimes saw it to be. On the occasion of Luther's 500th birthday in 1983, the government of the communist German Democratic Republic even issued a book hailing Luther's genuine achievements in the Reformation period. Some would say cynically that this was only done to promote tourism to the Luther shrines, but it is a change that would have been unthinkable from that government a few decades ago.

Many new contacts, which you will read about in this book, are taking place where committed Christians and committed Marxists come together for study and for dialogue. Whether this happens in a university in Czechoslovakia, a village in Tanzania, a city in Latin America, or even in a church conference in the United States, it is a challenging experience of unlocking the cupboard, often as frightening and unsettling for the doctrinaire Marxist as for the dogmatically certain Christian.

Sometimes those dialogues take place not between persons but within a single self, for one of the realities of the world today is that whether or not it is theoretically possible to be both a Christian and a Marxist, many, many people claim to be both. A *third hope* for readers of this book, then, is *learning something about the dialogue between Christianity and Marxism in our time.*

The Quest for Hope

Much of Marx's original impact came in his ability to give those who felt *stuck* in history a vision of what was happening and why. From that vision it was possible to move to action—not only to study the world and understand it, but also to change it.

It seemed to us in our study that Marxism is a remarkable phenomenon in our time for its continuing ability to generate hope among those people who so easily think of themselves as victims and losers in history. Americans in Vietnam, confronting a determined enemy, were surprised to discover that a Marxist vision of the world and its future could generate commitment as great as that held by those who believe in the Christian God and love America.

This is a most important *fourth hope* for readers of the book: *learning something about the dynamic character of Marxism which generates hope in the face of suffering and injustice.* Most readers of this book will agree that there is great suffering and injustice in our world today, and that the world needs a method to look to a hopeful future for life on this planet. But it may be a surprise for some to learn that Marxism or socialism seems to offer more hope for many people than, for example, the Christian faith or a capitalist economic system.

It will emerge in later chapters that the hope Marxists know differs sharply from classic Christian hope and yet has a historical relationship to Christian hope. The reader of this book may end up dismissing Marxism, even though she or he may at the end know more about it than at the beginning. But we think every reader will be pressed on the matter of hope to explain what—if not this Marxist vision in its various forms—can be offered to poor and oppressed people today, in our nation and elsewhere.

Unlocking the Bookcase

I haven't been back to the Fremont library for a while, so I don't know whether books about communism are in general circulation today, or whether they remain in the glass case. But I do know the authors of this book are diverse people who have studied Marxism together and who do not completely agree among themselves about its nature or its promise for humanity. But one point of agreement that made the writing possible was a common conviction—deeply shared—that the encounter with Marxism is a crucially important one for Christians today.

That encounter will require patience because much of what we must explain, especially in Marx's own thought, is extremely difficult to understand. The encounter will require courage, in the sense that any journey into another world of thought should challenge us to look critically at our own beliefs.

But we have studied and written with the conviction that our readers will possess the patience, courage, and curiosity needed to examine a world that many of us have seen only from afar. We believe that this bookcase of the many faces of Marxism ought to be unlocked, and that the contents ought to be taken out for examination.

Marx: The Man
and His Thought

1 The Life of Karl Marx

by Wayne C. Stumme

For Marx was above all else a revolutionist. His real mission in life was to contribute, in one way or another, to the overthrow of capitalist society and of the state institutions which it had brought into being, to contribute to the liberation of the modern proletariat, which *he* was the first to make conscious of its own position and its needs, conscious of the conditions of its emancipation. Fighting was his element. And he fought with a passion, a tenacity and a success such as few could rival.[1]

Speech by Engels
at the graveside of Marx

The Early Years (1818-1843)

On May 5, 1818, in the ancient city of Trier in the Prussian Rhineland, a child was born whose thought and activity would influence world history for generations to come. By some he would be praised and followed, by others he would be condemned and avoided. More than any other individual, however, he kindled the revolutionary spirit of the 20th century, and the promise and the threat of contemporary existence, at least in part, can be traced to him.

Karl was the first son and the third of nine children born to Heinrich and Henriette Marx. Both parents were descendants of illustrious Jewish families and counted many well-known rabbis among their ancestors. Heinrich had broken with Judaism at an early age and, when the Rhineland had been ceded to Prussia at the conclusion of the Napoleonic

Wars, had accepted Baptism in order to remain as legal counsel in the regional government. Trier was a staunchly Catholic town, and the Marx family became part of a Lutheran community numbering no more than 200 persons. With respect both to his Jewishness and his Protestant affiliation, the young Karl was to experience the alienation of minority identification.

Karl, together with his brothers and sisters, was baptized in 1824. His mother received Baptism a year later. He enrolled in the Friedrich-Wilhelm Gymnasium in 1830, and there he was instructed in the Christian faith as it had been influenced by the ideas of the Enlightenment. The religious convictions of Karl's father were essentially deistic, and in a letter to his son he summed up his own outlook on life:

> A good support for morality is a simple faith in God. You know that I am the last person to be a fanatic. But sooner or later a man has a real need of this faith, and there are moments in life when even the man who denies God is compelled against his will to pray to the Almighty . . . everyone should submit to what was the faith of Newton, Locke, and Leibnitz.[2]

The views of Heinrich undoubtedly influenced his son, who maintained an affectionate relationship with his father until the latter's death.

Karl was required to write several essays as part of his school-leaving examination. His essay on religion dealt with "the reason, nature, necessity and effects of the union of believers with Christ" according to John 15:1-14. He argued that such union was necessary since without Christ persons could not reach the goal of salvation.[3] His strong interest in ethical questions was also evident in this paper. In March 1834 he was confirmed by his religion teacher, Pastor Joseph Kuepper.

The same spirit of Christian humanism marked his second essay, entitled "Reflections of a Youth on Choosing an Occupation." Its concluding words anticipate directions which Marx's thought would later take:

> History calls those the greatest men who ennobled themselves by working for the universal. Experience praises as the most happy the one who made the most people happy. Religion itself teaches us that the ideal for which we are all striving sacrificed itself for humanity, and who would dare to destroy such a statement.
>
> When we have chosen the vocation in which we can contribute most to humanity, burdens cannot bend us because they are only sacrifices for

all. Then we experience no meager, limited, egoistic joy, but our happiness belongs to millions, our deeds live on quietly but eternally effective, and glowing tears of noble men will fall on our ashes.[4]

In the autumn of 1835 Marx matriculated at the University of Bonn as a student of law. His considerable range of extracurricular activities brought him into sizeable debt. An interest in the writing of poetry resulted in literary works which his father neither understood nor appreciated. One year at Bonn was enough; Heinrich Marx approved of his son's transfer to the more cosmopolitan University of Berlin in the fall of 1836.

Before leaving for Berlin, Marx became engaged to his childhood sweetheart and neighbor, Jenny von Westphalen. She belonged to a family of Prussian aristocrats which had ties to Scottish nobility. Four years older than Karl, Jenny entered the relationship despite the misgivings of some members of her family. Much of Marx's time at the university would be given to letters and poems dedicated to Jenny.

Marx remained at Berlin for four and one-half years. His romantic interest in poetry lasted for only a brief period. Marx found philosophy displacing the study of law as a vocational interest, and he came under the influence of the idealistic philosophies of Fichte and Kant. At first he rejected the rationalistic philosophy of Georg Wilhelm Friedrich Hegel—whose views were dominant in Berlin until his death in 1831— but finally Marx was won over by the philosopher's comprehensive view of history and its ongoing transformation. As he was to do throughout his life, Marx sought to clarify his thinking in an extensive paper which he called "Cleanthes, or the Starting Point and the Necessary Progress of Philosophy."

His conversion to Hegel's thought was complete. Marx soon joined a group known as the Young Hegelians, who attacked the various orthodoxies of the time and particularly religion. Contrary to Hegel himself, who was a practicing Lutheran, these radical disciples rejected all religious belief as outdated. From theological criticism they proceeded to political criticism, a more dangerous activity in conservative and repressive Prussia. Marx and other "left-wing" Hegelians formed an association known as the Doctor's Club, and in that setting he began to work out his own understanding of philosophy and society. A satiric poem by another club member offers this description of Marx during this period:

But who advances here full of impetuosity?
It is a dark form from Trier, an unleashed monster,

> With self-assured step he hammers the ground with his heels
> And raises his arms in full fury to heaven
> As though he wished to seize the celestial vault
>   and lower it to earth.[5]

His new views and activities led to increased tension with his family. Letters from his father reveal his displeasure, although the bonds which united the two were never threatened. In May of 1838 Heinrich Marx died. His son had been a source of pride and a cause of deep distress. Marx always remembered his father with affection, and carried with him throughout his life an old daguerreotype photograph of Heinrich. At Marx's death, Engels placed the picture in his coffin.

Marx began work on his doctoral thesis in 1839. His subject was the thought of Epicurus, an ancient Greek moral philosopher. As a result of his study he was able to distance himself from aspects of Hegel's thought. Marx was fascinated by the mythical figure of Prometheus, who defied the gods by bringing the gift of fire to humanity. His notes for the thesis show that his break with the Christian faith of his youth was complete:

> . . . the proofs for the existence of God are nothing but *proofs for the existence of the essentially human self-consciousness and logical explanations of it.*[6]

Submitting his thesis to the University of Jena, Marx was granted his doctoral diploma on April 15, 1841.

Marx's unorthodox views prevented him from securing a teaching post and his friends encouraged him to turn to political journalism. In the spring of 1842 Marx began to write for a liberal, middle-class newspaper known as the *Rheinische Zeitung*. He moved to Cologne in October and took over as editor-in-chief. Here he met for the first time Friedrich Engels, who was to become his lifelong collaborator and friend. Vigorously expressing his radical views, Marx came into conflict with both the newspaper's shareholders and the government censors, and he resigned his post in March 1843.

Marx had now been engaged for more than seven years. Jenny and her mother had moved to the resort town of Kreuznach 50 miles east of Trier. Confessing to a friend that he was "head-over-heels in love," Marx made plans with Jenny for a summer wedding. On June 19, 1843, they were married in the Lutheran church and registry office in Kreuznach. They spent their honeymoon in Switzerland and then returned for several months to Kreuznach. During this time Marx completed his essay *On the Jewish Question* in which he finally broke with the idealistic notions of the state which he had taken over from Hegel.

The time of preparation for his revolutionary vocation had come to an end. Karl Marx was about to begin the work which would transform the scattered and weak associations of European workers into a powerful movement for extensive social change.

Years of European Engagement (1843-1849)

Paris had become the center for expatriate German radicals. The German publicist Arnold Ruge, an admirer of the intellectual and journalistic gifts of Marx, invited him to become coeditor of a Paris-based journal to be called the *Deutsch-Franzoesische Jahrbuecher*. Marx quickly accepted the offer, and he and Jenny arrived in Paris in October 1843. She already was pregnant with their first child.

Marx's contributions to the annual exhibited his concern with the division between state and society and the consequent inability of liberal politics to provide solutions for social problems. In addition to his essay *On the Jewish Question,* he published an introduction to a critique of the political philosophy of Hegel. This brief yet significant paper contained ideas which were to come to fuller expression in Marx's later writings. He set forth his negative view of religion and his hope for human emancipation in vigorous and compelling language, and he pointed to the working classes—the so-called proletariat—as the historical agent of society's transformation.

Marx did not limit his Paris relationships to the socialist intellectuals gathered there, but associated frequently with workers and artisans. He recorded his impression of the latter in the *Economic and Philosophical Manuscripts* compiled during this period:

> When communist *artisans* form associations, teaching and propaganda are their first aims. But their association itself creates a new need—the need for society—and what appears to be a means has become an end. The most striking results of this practical development are to be seen when French socialist workers meet together . . . the brotherhood of man is no empty phrase but a reality, and the nobility of man shines forth upon us from their toil-worn bodies.[7]

The need for a society in which such workers did not live as alienated and oppressed individuals increasingly dominated the thinking of Marx. More and more his study, writing, and political activity came to focus on this concern.

The increasingly radical ideas of Marx finally led to a break in his relations with Ruge. The *Jahrbuecher* failed after a single issue, and the two men ended their association. The journal had already been banned in Prussia where its distinctively socialist position was considered seditious. In a letter written to the philosopher Feuerbach during this time, Ruge offered a not entirely objective description of Marx:

> He reads a great deal, works with unusual intensity and possesses a critical ability which sometimes degenerates into arrogant dialectics; but he does not finish anything, continually breaks off that which he is working on and plunges time and again into an endless sea of books.[8]

In May of 1844 a daughter, Jenny, was born to the Marx family. An August visit by Friedrich Engels inaugurated the cooperation between the two men and marked the beginning of a unique friendship. Engels, then working in his father's factory in England, would come again and again to the financial aid of the Marx family in the years ahead. Engels' book, *The Condition of the Working Class in England,* published in 1845, made a favorable impression on Marx. Communist by conviction and capitalist by occupation, Engels experienced the tensions of his dual role throughout his long association with Marx.

By the beginning of 1845 the French government, under pressure from Prussia, had decided to expel Marx and other radical German expatriates. The Marx family moved to Brussels, their home until March of 1848. Belgium granted Marx political asylum on the condition that he refrain from political activity.

Marx, frequently consulting with Engels, took up the study of economic theory. The writings of early French socialists and the English economists were of particular interest to him. He presented his own understanding of socialism in the polemical work *The Holy Family.* His views of class conflict underwent further development and took on sharper focus.

> The possessing class and the proletarian class represent one and the same human self-alienation. But the former feels satisfied and affirmed in this self-alienation, experiences the alienation as a sign of *its own power,* and possesses in it the *appearance* of a human existence. The latter, however, feels destroyed in this alienation, seeing in it its own impotence and the reality of an inhuman existence.[9]

It was during these years in Belgium that Marx articulated his concept of historical materialism, a key notion in the growing self-consciousness of the European working classes.

In September of 1845 a second child, Laura, was born to Jenny and Karl Marx. The family also grew when Jenny's mother sent Helene Demuth, a servant in the von Westphalen household, to help with the domestic tasks. Leni or Lenchen, as she was called, was to share the life of the Marx family throughout the years of exile in Europe and England.

By 1846 Marx and Engels had succeeded in establishing a network of international correspondence committees. Their intention was to link the industrial proletariat in various countries in order that the exchange of ideas might prepare the workers for the anticipated revolutionary changes. Marx's literary efforts during this period, moreover, were concerned with the readiness of the proletariat for what he considered their historic role. He wanted to provide them with an adequate basis for their actions, that is, a social analysis and a political program. These ideas were included in a work known as *The German Ideology,* which, though not published during his lifetime, advanced many of the views he was to develop in later years.

In December 1846 Edgar was born into a family whose financial situation was becoming desperate. Marx and Jenny nevertheless held things together with courage and good humor. A visitor to their Brussels home reported this observation:

> I have seldom known so happy a marriage in which joy and suffering—the latter in most abundant measure—were shared and all sorrow overcome in the consciousness of full and mutual dependency.[10]

Another guest during this time, the Russian Paul Annenkov, gave this description of Marx:

> Marx himself was the type of man who is made up of energy, will and unshakable conviction. He was most remarkable in his appearance. He had a shock of deep black hair and hairy hands and his coat was buttoned wrong; but he looked like a man who had the right and power to demand respect, no matter how he appeared before you and no matter what he did. . . . He always spoke in imperative words that would brook no contradiction and were made all the sharper by the almost painful expression of tone which ran through everything he said. This tone expressed the firm conviction of his mission to dominate men's minds and prescribe

them their laws. Before me stood the embodiment of a democratic dictator such as one might imagine in a day dream.[11]

In 1847 a worker's organization called the League of the Just issued an invitation for an international congress to be held that summer in London. Engels attended. The congress in London formed a new movement known as the Communist League. Marx and Engels became members of the League, and later in the year Marx attended its second congress. While in England he met privately with the leaders of various English associations of workers. The time was critical for the proletarian movement. All European countries were suffering from a severe economic depression, and the growing restiveness of the working classes and the peasants seemed to signal the anticipated social upheaval for which the movement was waiting.

The second meeting of the Communist League had charged Marx and Engels with the responsibility for producing a "manifesto" which would make the views of the working class movement more widely known. Earlier drafts were prepared by Engels, but he acknowledged that the final *Communist Manifesto* was "essentially Marx's work." Published in London in early 1848 by the Working Men's Educational Association, it was both a reasoned and passionate call to action directed toward the oppressed working classes. Given the volatile social setting of mid-century Europe, it was an unmistakable summons to revolution.

With this pamphlet Marx established his reputation as the leading theoretician of the movement. A sympathetic contemporary recalled his impression of the young Marx:

> Marx was then still a young man, about 28 years old, but he greatly impressed us all. He was of medium height, broad-shouldered, powerful in build, and vigorous in his movements. His forehead was high and finely shaped, his hair thick and pitch-black, his gaze piercing. His mouth already had the sarcastic curl that his opponents feared so much. Marx was a born leader of the people. His speech was brief, convincing and compelling in its logic. He never said a superfluous word; every sentence contained an idea and every idea was an essential link in the chain of his argument.[12]

Marx was expelled from Belgium in early March of 1848 because of his political activity. At the same time the provisional French government invited him to return to Paris. There he began to set up the central office of the Communist League and also encouraged the expatriate Germans to return to their homeland. The unrest of the workers was growing. In country after country workers and peasants were demonstrating and, in some instances, rioting. In May 1848 Marx and Engels traveled to Cologne, the third largest city in Prussia, and began publication of a radical newspaper, the *Neue Rheinische Zeitung*. Marx's inflammatory articles intensified the antagonism between the German workers and the feudal-absolutist elements in the society. Revolution seemed to be in the air.

Events came to a head in early 1849 when Marx and others were brought to trial by the Cologne authorities for inciting the workers to rebellion. Marx spoke in his own defense and, though he was acquitted of the charges against him, he finally was expelled from Prussian territory by the government in May. Returning to Paris, Marx and his family found themselves without financial resources. Their friends arranged a collection, and they were able to leave 'for England. There Marx, with the exception of brief trips to the continent, was to remain for the rest of his life.

Early Years in England (1850-1856)

The early years in England were desperately hard years for the Marx family. Their continuing financial problems made the transition to English life most difficult. Two rooms at 64 Dean Street was their first home in London, and a short time later they moved to number 28 on the same street. Their son Guido, born shortly after their arrival in England, died suddenly from meningitis. For a time Marx thought of emigrating to the United States together with Engels, but he soon concluded that such a move was beyond his means.

Still believing that a European revolution was imminent, Marx and Engels started a political journal known as the *Neue Rheinische Zeitung Revue*. Now Marx began to develop his earlier ideas in relation to more recent European events. Particularly important from this period were his essays on *The Class Struggle in France* (1850) and *The Eighteenth Brumaire of Louis Bonaparte* (1852). In these writings he demonstrated his insight into contemporary movements and his outstanding theoretical skills.

London was a place of relative freedom in comparison with the generally repressive atmosphere prevailing elsewhere in Europe. Political refugees and dissidents from throughout the continent made their way there, and Marx lost little time in establishing contact with them. His special interest was German workers, whom he taught frequently with respect to their role in the coming transformation of European society.

One of Marx's lecture sessions has been described by Wilhelm Lieb-knecht, a founder of the German socialist party.

> Marx proceeded methodically. He stated a proposition—the shorter the better—and then demonstrated it in a lengthier explanation, endeavoring with utmost care to avoid all expressions incomprehensible to the workers. Then he requested his audience to put questions to him. If this was not done he commenced to examine the workers, and he did this with such pedagogic skill that no flaw, no misunderstanding, escaped him. On expressing my surprise about his dexterity I learned that Marx had for-merly given lectures on political economy in the worker's club in Brus-sels. At all events he had the qualities of a good teacher. He also made use of a blackboard, on which he wrote the formulas—among them those familiar to all of us from the beginning of *Capital*.[13]

In addition to his journalistic and educational activities, Marx began a program of intensive study in economic history and theory. For years to come he would carry on this work in the library of the British Mu-seum. He had already determined that he would prepare a major study dealing with industrial capitalism, and he asked his friends to help him find an interested publisher.

Regular gifts from Engels were not enough to ease the persisting poverty of the Marx household. The birth of another daughter, Fran-ziska, in March 1851, put another strain on the family's meager re-sources. In June of the same year the family servant, Helene Demuth, gave birth to a son, Frederick. Engels acknowledged paternity and took over all expenses for the child, who was removed from the Dean Street residence and raised in a foster family. Later documents named Marx as the father of the boy. Marx described these difficult times in a letter to Engels.

> For about the past fortnight now I have written absolutely nothing, for when I am not at the library I am hunted like a dog and therefore, despite the best intentions, I am constantly interrupted in my work . . . at home disruptions and disturbances are too much for me. Everything is constantly in a state of siege and the streams of tears for nights on end try my nerves and drive me mad. Naturally I cannot do much. I feel sorry for my wife. She has the heaviest load to bear.[14]

In August of 1851 the liberal American newspaper, the *New York Daily Tribune*, engaged Marx as its European correspondent. He was to depend upon this work as a source of income for a number of years, although Engels would write many of the articles published under his name. During this time Jenny began to help Marx with his voluminous correspondence, and she also took responsibility for transcribing into legible script his almost undecipherable writing. Marx acknowledged the loyal and unselfish support of his wife and of his best friend Engels, and he continued to depend upon their help for the remainder of his working life.

The destitution of the Marx family deepened during these early years in England. Franziska died of bronchitis when she was a year old, and Jenny had to borrow money from their French neighbors to pay for a coffin and burial. Marx frequently would pawn his clothes in order to buy food for the family. His efforts to find additional employment were unsuccessful. Marx suffered from hepatitis and other chronic illnesses, and Jenny and the children were often in poor health. Money for medicine and a doctor was simply not available.

The youngest Marx child, Eleanor, was born in January 1855. She soon contracted a serious illness but survived. Eight year old Edgar was less fortunate. In March he suffered a gastric fever and on April 6, 1855, he died in his father's arms. The "animating spirit" of the Marx household was gone, and Karl and Jenny were desolate. Marx, who rarely expressed his personal feelings, spoke of his anguish in a letter to Engels:

> The house is naturally utterly desolate and forlorn since the death of the dear child who was its living soul. It is impossible to describe how we miss him at every turn. I have suffered every kind of misfortune, but I have only just learned what real unhappiness is.[15]

By 1856 the family, aided by an inheritance from Jenny's family, was able to move into more spacious quarters in the Maitland Park area of London.

The revolutionary unrest of 1848-1849 had by now been quieted by the counterrevolutionary force of the traditional European leadership. The Communist League had split into quarreling factions and then disbanded. A related group, the Universal Society of Communist Revolutionaries, also came to an end. Marx and his colleagues, however, doggedly continued to work for the goals they had set when the League and the Society had come into being.

> The aim of the society is the overthrow of all the privileged classes, and to submit these classes to the dictatorship of the proletariat by maintaining the revolution in permanence until the realization of communism, which will be the last organizational form of the human family.[16]

From their perspective, the ascendency of the powers of social reaction was only temporary; the tide of history was running in the direction of the workers' movement. Their weakness and disunity would be overcome, for the future belonged to those who struggled to free the proletariat from "capital and wage slavery."

The Study of Political Economy (1857-1863)

A general European recession spurred Marx on as he sought to understand the economic basis of social and political change. His studies, carried on with scientific rigor and incredible diligence, were intended to provide a theoretical basis for the political activity of the European working classes. The range of Marx's reading was immense: he was interested not only in the classical economists but in philosophy, history, anthropology, literature, mathematics, natural science, and contemporary political and military events.

By 1858 Marx had completed the introductory work for his proposed study of capitalist economics. Not published until after his death, these preparatory notes were entitled *Outlines for a Critique of Political Economy or the Grundrisse.* Many of the emphases which received fuller treatment in the later *Capital* were anticipated in this earlier writing. These views were developed in close collaboration with Engels, and Marx also consulted with the German socialist leader, Ferdinand Lassalle.

The financial difficulties of the Marx family had now reached crisis proportions. Engels, who had come to the family's rescue on numerous other occasions, promised Marx that he would make contributions of at least five pounds a month to their needs. Both Marx and his wife were in poor health, and the growing requirements of keeping the children fed and clothed and in school added to their anxiety. Marx was regularly besieged by creditors demanding payment. His family situation affected Marx's ability to concentrate effort on his project in economic theory. Jenny described matters in a letter to a friend:

> Mental unrest and turbulence due to his inability to complete his work quickly and without interruptions naturally worsen his physical condition; the same applies to the onerous tasks necessary to earn his daily bread and they, of course, cannot be pushed aside.[17]

Marx's only assured income during this period came from the *New York Daily Tribune,* which paid him for the more than 60 articles he (or

Engels) wrote as the newspaper's European correspondent. His journalistic efforts strongly criticized the imperialistic ventures of England, greeted the emancipation of the Russian serfs as "the beginning of true civilization in Russia,"[18] and attacked the reactionary policies of Napoleon III in France while welcoming the political changes which were taking place in Italy and Germany.

The year 1859 was marked by the publication of John Stuart Mill's influential book *On Liberty* and Charles Darwin's epoch-creating work *Origin of Species*. At the same time Marx's *Critique of Political Economy* was printed, and its well-known preface gave concise expression to the materialist understanding of history. His efforts were largely ignored by his contemporaries, although they would later be read for the clues they gave to his more technical writings. His studies in political economy, to which he returned whenever possible, were interrupted by the need to defend himself against attacks from within and outside the workers' movement. Old and valued friendships were strained, sometimes broken, and, from time to time, restored. Relations with the influential German socialist Ferdinand Lassalle, for instance, were threatened both by personal and professional differences.

Following the outbreak of the American Civil War, Marx's income from his journalistic work declined sharply. The family continued to be plagued with sickness and debt, as Marx disclosed in a letter to Engels.

> How I am supposed to carry on here I do not know, for taxes, school, house, grocer, butcher, God and the devil don't want to give me any further respite. . . . I don't know what I should do, but I have seen this crisis approaching for some time now.[19]

The situation was temporarily eased when his relatives in Holland gave him an advance on the inheritance he expected from his mother. During a trip to the continent in 1861, Marx visited Lassalle in Berlin (his reactions to the visit were mixed), his mother in Trier, and his Dutch relatives.

Intensely interested in the American Civil War, Marx analyzed the conflict as a struggle between antagonistic social systems. The English economy was affected by the war, and Engels, who was still working for his father in Manchester, was unable to help the Marx family as generously as before. The plight of Marx and Jenny and the children became steadily worse, and Marx described his wife's suffering to

Engels:

> My wife tells me every day that she would prefer lying with the children in the grave and, indeed, I cannot blame her for feeling so for the humiliations, anguish and fear which must be withstood are truly indescribable.[20]

Despite these difficulties, Marx continued to study and write. His *Theories of Surplus Value* was published in 1862, and he made steady progress on the massive work which would be known as *Capital*. Near the end of 1863 Marx received news of his mother's death and traveled to Trier in order to settle questions of inheritance. Before returning to England, he visited for an extensive period in the home of his Dutch relatives who tended his chronic and painful skin disease.

The First International (1864-1872)

The two legacies that came in early 1864 marked a turning point for the Marx family. They were able to move into a more comfortable home in the same part of northwest London. The years of privation, however, had taken their toll, and Marx never regained full health. Time after time he would have to interrupt his work on *Capital* in order to recuperate, but illness could not compel him to abandon what had become his life's work.

In October 1864 Marx gave the inaugural address at the organizing meeting of the Working Men's International Association, more popularly known as the First International. The association represented the culmination of the workers' activities since the revolutionary years of 1848-1849, and Marx did not hesitate from reminding his hearers that "to conquer political power has become the great duty of the working classes."[21] As he reviewed the past and set forth the directions for the new organization, Marx did not emphasize the revolutionary character of the historical vocation of the proletariat. Marx was elected a member of the General Council of the International which, despite its obvious respect for him, was far from being an exclusively socialist organization.

In the years that followed, Marx put much time and energy into the work of the International. Factional fighting (to which he contributed on more than one occasion) accounted for much of its initially slow progress. Nevertheless, despite the hardships experienced by the International, Marx was sustained by his conviction that the instincts of the proletarian masses could be trusted. As he saw it, his task was to help bring to conscious awareness the theoretical understanding which the working classes required. Marx believed that without this understanding their efforts to achieve social change would lack direction and effectiveness. Largely due to the work of Marx and his collaborators, the International was an acknowledged power on the European scene by the end of the 1860s.

The Russian anarchist and sometime supporter of Marx, Michael Bakunin, has left a description in which the tensions between the two men are apparent:

> We see each other fairly often and I very much admired him for his knowledge and for his passionate devotion to the cause of the proletariat, although it always had in it an admixture of personal vanity; and I eagerly sought his conversation, which was instructive and witty so long as it was not inspired by petty spite—which, unfortunately, happened too often. But there was never real intimacy between us. Our temperaments did not harmonize. He called me a sentimental idealist; and he was right. I called him vain, treacherous and morose, and I too was right.[22]

Other contemporaries also noted the single mindedness and combativeness of Marx when it came to the cause of the proletariat. Others who knew him well offered contrasting opinions. In her reminiscences, Marx's daughter Eleanor wrote:

> To those who knew Karl Marx no legend is funnier than the common one which pictures him a morose, bitter, unbending, unapproachable man. . . . This picture of the cheeriest, gayest soul that ever breathed, of a man brimming over with humor and good-humor, whose hearty laugh was infectious and irresistable, of the kindliest, gentlest, most sympathetic of companions, is a standing wonder—and amusement—to those who knew him.
>
> In his home life, as in his intercourse with friends, and even with mere acquaintances, I think one might say that Karl Marx's main characteristics were his unbounded good-humor and his unlimited sympathy. His kindness and patience were really sublime. A less sweet-tempered man would have often been driven frantic by the constant interruptions, the continual demands made upon him by all sorts of people.[23]

During 1865 Marx delivered his lectures on "Wages, Price, and Profit" to the General Council of the International. These anticipated his theories about industrial capitalism which finally appeared in the first volume of *Capital*. Published in 1867, this was the only volume of his major work to be completed during his lifetime. The remaining two volumes appeared after his death, and were readied for publication only after a massive effort on the part of Engels. Marx himself said that he had sacrificed "health, happiness, and family" to the completion of *Capital*, the work that was to constitute the permanent basis for his reputation as political economist and social theorist.

The Marx family was not free of financial worries during this period. Their inheritances were consumed by expenses related to Karl's work and the needs of their growing children. Karl and Jenny were determined that their daughters secure good educations and contract suitable marriages. As he had done so often in the past, Friedrich Engels gave generous assistance to the family. Burdened by overwork and weakened by illness, Marx refused to give up his responsibilities in the working men's movement. At the same time he engaged in extensive research as background for his economic writings.

By 1870 Karl and Jenny had become grandparents for the second time. That year also marked the outbreak of the Franco-Prussian War, which Marx saw as an instrument of Bismarck's expansionist policies and a serious threat to the solidarity of European workers. Marx vacillated in his attitudes toward the war, but an event following the French defeat called forth his last great political pamphlet, *The Civil War in France*. That event was the brutal repression of the Paris Commune in 1871 by the French provisional government. Marx's pamphlet was read to the General Council of the International only two days after the last resistance of the workers had been crushed, and it described the slaughter as a "mute but eloquent testimony to the frenzy of which the ruling class is capable as soon as the working class dares to stand up for its rights."[24] Marx led efforts to provide help for the refugees from Paris who were able to reach London.

The International was plagued with increasing internal dissension. Marx and the alleged "authoritarianism" of the General Council came under frequent attack, particularly from the anarchist faction led by Michael Bakunin. The growing crisis prompted Marx and Engels to prepare and circulate a private manifesto in early 1872. The General Council adopted and published this paper, entitled "Alleged Splits in the International," in which anarchism was presented as destructive of the working men's movement. Exhausted by work and these conflicts, Marx resigned from the General Council at its September 1872 congress at the Hague. The decision to move the General Council to New York signaled the approaching end of the First International. For Marx himself the struggle was far from over; his closing words to the congress echoed his lifelong commitment:

> The rest of my life will be dedicated as all my past effort has been, to the triumph of the social ideas which some day—and let us hold this one conviction—will bring about the universal rule of the proletariat.[25]

The Final Years (1873-1883)

Although Marx continued to work on the unpublished volumes of *Capital* and kept up an extensive correspondence, the final decade of his life produced little in the way of major writings. His health continued to deteriorate. On an almost daily basis, Marx suffered from chronic hepatitis, bronchial infections, skin ailments, and high blood pressure. Jenny's health was also failing, and their youngest daughter Eleanor nursed both parents through their final years. The burdens of their literary collaboration were assumed increasingly by Friedrich Engels, who also vigorously defended Marx against the verbal assaults of his enemies on the political right and left.

From time to time Marx would interrupt his research and writing for brief trips to the seaside or European spas. The temporary relief he sometimes gained did not halt the steady decline in his physical powers. In 1874 the death of a grandson, Jenny's child, saddened both Marx and his wife. He expressed his sorrow in a letter to his daughter.

> The house is dead now, since the little angel no longer fills it with life. I miss him at every step. It hurts me so to think of him and yet how can one banish from one's mind the thought of such a sweet, fine little fellow. But I do hope, my child, that to please your old father, you are keeping up your courage.[26]

Marx's love of children, more poignant because of the early death of three of his own, was noted by several of his contemporaries. His daughter recorded that what Marx liked best about Jesus was his love of children. Christianity, she had heard him say, could be forgiven much because it taught the love of children.[27]

In 1875 the German socialists met at Gotha where they were able to unite their opposing factions and adopt a common program. Both Marx and Engels felt it necessary to criticize the document, noting that it had not included the "first condition of all freedom: that all functionaries be responsible for all their official actions to every citizen before the ordinary courts and according to normal law."[28] Marx's comments were published by Engels in 1891 and represented a detailed analysis of the programmatic issues relating to a workers' party.

During these last years Marx concerned himself increasingly with Russia and its potential for social revolution. He was aware that the first volume of *Capital,* in Bakunin's translation, was widely read in Russia and had considerable influence in revolutionary circles. Revising somewhat his theory that social revolution required a developed bourgeois society, Marx suggested that the archaic village commune of Russia could well become "the mainspring of Russia's social regeneration" in the process of transformation into a socialist society.[29]

Weakened by recurrent illnesses, worn out by extensive political and literary work during the years of poverty, Marx nevertheless continued to maintain an active interest in the cause of the proletariat. Something of that commitment can be sensed in this description by the English social reformer Henry Mayers Hyndman of Marx in his final years:

> The first impression of Marx as I saw him was that of a powerful, shaggy, untamed old man, ready, not to say eager, to enter into conflict and rather suspicious himself of immediate attack. . . . He turned from the role of prophet and vehement denunciator to that of calm philosopher without any apparent effort, and I felt from the first that on this latter ground many a long year might pass before I ceased to be a student in the presence of a master.[30]

Jenny was the first to succumb. Suffering from cancer, she was confined to her room. Marx was in an adjacent room recovering from bronchitis. Their daughter Eleanor later recalled their final days together:

> It was a terrible time. Our dear mother lay in the big front room, Moor (the family's nickname for Karl) in the small room behind. And the two of them, who were so used to one another, so close to one another, could not even be together in the same room. . . .
> Never shall I forget the morning when he felt strong enough to go into Mother's room. When they were together they were young again— she a young girl and he a loving youth, both on the threshold of life, not an old man devastated by illness and an old dying woman parting from each other forever.[31]

Jenny died on December 2, 1881. Marx was unable to attend the funeral where the eulogy was delivered by Engels.

Jenny's death was a blow from which Marx never recovered. His health worsened, and trips abroad no longer gave temporary respite. On March 14, 1883, Karl Marx died in the study of his Maitland Park home. It was Engel's task to notify the leaders of the workers' movement of his death. Writing to the German socialist Eduard Bernstein, Engels summed up the significance of Marx for the proletarian cause:

> Only one who was constantly with him can imagine what this man was worth to us as a theorist and at all decisive moments in practical matters as well. . . . The movement will take its course, but it will miss the calm, timely, and considered intervention which has saved it hitherto from many a wrong and wearisome path.[32]

On March 17, Karl Marx was buried at Highgate Cemetery in north London. Engels gave the final tribute. His closing words reflected the convictions of many in the movement Marx did so much to create:

> He died beloved, revered and mourned by millions of revolutionary fellow workers—from the mines of Siberia to California, in all parts of Europe and America—and I make bold to say that though he may have had many opponents he had hardly one personal enemy.
> His name will endure through the ages, and so also will his work![33]

2 Marx's Thought: Human Nature and Destiny

by Ronald F. Thiemann

Marxism is an international movement with an extraordinary variety of expressions. Often it is difficult to see what principles the Maoism of China holds in common with the Democratic Socialism of the Frankfurt School. Yet Marxists of every stripe and description appeal to Karl Marx as the source and norm for their brand of Marxism. If we hope to view Marxism's "many faces," then it seems wise to begin our study with a careful look at the thought of the man who spawned the movement which bears his name. Marx's writings are difficult and complex, and they treat a wide range of topics, only a few of which we can discuss in these chapters. Like all important thinkers Marx has received diverse and often conflicting interpretations, especially at the hands of those who have wanted to use his thought to support or oppose a particular program. No attempt will be made here to sort through the welter of claims and counterclaims produced by interpreters of Marx. Rather, we want to introduce a few central ideas in Marx's thought so that the overall pattern of his thinking might become clear.

Most of the writings from which these ideas are drawn were written early in Marx's career. Especially important among these early documents is the *Economic and Philosophical Manuscripts* written in Paris in 1844. We are emphasizing these early writings for a number of reasons. First, the early writings show most clearly the moral and philosophical roots of Marx's vision of human nature and destiny. That vision is apt to be overlooked if one concentrates on the later writings such as *The Communist Manifesto* and *Capital*. Marx's supporters and opponents in their zeal to *use* Marx for some political end often ignore the deep moral humanism which fires Marx's early writings. Second, those thinkers who have attempted to combine Marxism with democratic principles (see especially Chapter 8) have been most deeply influenced by the early Marx. These are the persons with whom Christians have been in dialogue, and the greatest hope for mutual understanding and rapprochement between Marxists and Christians would seem to depend upon a common understanding of these earliest writings. Finally, it seems especially important that American Christians study Marx in his most persuasive and challenging writings. Too often people are swayed into accepting or rejecting a caricature of Marx, a caricature perpetuated by supporters and opponents alike. If Christians are to seriously consider Marxism, then we must study the most challenging writings produced by the founder of that movement. Because the early writings are both profoundly moral and sharply anti-Christian they deserve our close attention.

This chapter will focus on Marx's anthropology, that is, his view of human nature. The following chapter will show how his understanding of humanity resulted in his critique of religion.

Praxis: the Key Concept

Marx's view of human nature was developed in opposition to the predominant philosophical views of the 19th century. It was common for 19th-century philosophers to define the essence of human beings as consciousness or mind. They argued that the quality which most sharply distinguished humans from plants or other animals was the human ability to *think*. Philosophers as diverse as Plato, Descartes, and Hegel agreed that consciousness—the ability to think—was the essential human quality: To be is to think. Karl Marx, however, identified this assumption as the crucial *mistake* of all Western philosophy. "The philosophers have only *interpreted* the world in various ways," Marx wrote, "the point is, to *change* it."[1] If human beings were essentially *thinkers,* then all they could do would be to reflect upon or contemplate or interpret the world. The world itself—with its problems, evils, and injustices— would remain the same; what would change would simply be the way of thinking about it. If humans were merely thinkers, Marx argued, then they would never be actors. They would accept the world as it was, and fail to be agents for change.

But, wrote Marx, if the point of human life were to *change* the world, then the essence of human beings had to be defined as something other than consciousness or mind. Much of Marx's early thought was devoted to the project of overturning the dominant Western definition of humanity and replacing it with an anthropology oriented toward action. According to Marx, human beings were active, laboring, productive creatures. Humans were not primarily passive and contemplative but active and working: To be is to act, or better, to be is to work. A human being *is* what he or she *does*. Only if this definition of humanity was adopted, said Marx, would it be possible to be about the task of changing the world.

The key concept in Marx's new view of humanity was *praxis,* a Greek word which is usually translated as "activity" or "practice." Marx borrowed this term from ancient philosophy in order to stress the practical action-oriented nature of his thinking. But Marx radically reinterpreted the notion of *praxis,* and we need to look at the various ideas which are implied in the term.

Praxis is "sensuous human activity."[2] We have already seen that Marx defined humanity in terms of activity. The important new word introduced in the definition above is *sensuous.* According to Marx, sensuous activity was that which involved the human senses in interaction with the material world. Humans were most fully human when they used their senses to act in the world of nature. While traditional philosophers would have stressed the mind's contemplation of ideas, Marx emphasized the senses in interaction with the material of nature. Because of this concentration on the sensuous and the material, Marx is rightly called a "materialist." But the term simply indicates that Marx gave priority in his anthropology to the human senses and the material world.

It follows from the preceding definition of *praxis* that the basic form of human activity should be labor, the action of making products, i.e., of producing objects from the material of nature. "The worker can make nothing without *nature,* without the *sensuous external world.* It is the material wherein his labor realizes itself, wherein it is active, out of which and by means of which it produces."[3]

In thinking about the relation between labor and nature, Marx introduced one of his most important, although most difficult, ideas. When most people thought about the relation between a worker and the product he or she produced, they tended to make a sharp distinction between the person of the worker and the object produced. After all, Marx pointed out, the worker was a human subject, and the object was simply a thing. That common sense distinction between subject and object or worker and product had been accepted by most Western philosophy through the mid-19th century. But Marx wanted to challenge both the common sense distinction and its philosophical defense. Marx argued that the product or object was not simply external to and separated from the nature of the worker. People tended to think of the products of labor as external objects because they were led to think that way by a capitalist economy and its worship of private property. In fact, Marx argued, the products of labor were simply the objective form of the worker's human nature. If people *are* what they *do,* and if what humans did was to produce objects, then it followed that what they produced was in some sense the embodiment of who they were. "The object of labor is thus the objectification of man's species-life; he produces himself not only intellectually, as in consciousness, but also actually in a real sense and sees himself in a world he made."[4] Marx believed that as active beings humans externalized themselves through the objects they made, that is, they literally "poured themselves into" the products of their labor. The objects of our world are ours not in the sense that we possess them, but in the sense that those objects are nothing less than our human nature in objective form.

Perhaps a concrete example will help to clarify what Marx meant. Think of a small self-sufficient community in the backwoods of Maine. An artisan wants to build a set of wooden benches for the town church and meeting hall. To do so he needs the help of those who will cut the trees, trim the bark, saw the wood into suitable lengths, and deliver it to the artisan's workshop. The bench-building job is by its very nature a social activity. It requires the cooperation of others in the community in interaction with nature to accomplish the task. The artisan himself spends countless hours in fulfilling labor creating the benches. He "pours himself into" the task and gives his own unique touch to the creation of his product. When the task is done, the artisan sees the benches as an expression of his own nature, the objectified form of who he is. The artifacts or products are the externalized nature of the artisan or laborer. He does not own or possess the objects, because they were produced through a communal effort. The benches do not *belong* to him any more than the logs which the lumberman splits *belong* to him. The benches, like the trees from which they came, are held in common by the whole community and express the true nature of the community. The thought of selling the benches for money would hardly occur to the artisan. He simply helps others to move and install the benches in the meeting house, where they will be for the use and enjoyment of the whole community. Thus in their production and in their use the benches are the objective form of the artisan's own nature and in a larger sense an expression of the nature of the whole community.

This example highlights not only Marx's notion of products as objectified human nature but also Marx's social definition of humanity. According to Marx, the essential human activity was labor, and labor was always a *social* activity. Humans could not produce as isolated individuals. Production, as the example above shows, required a community that worked cooperatively to achieve a particular end. Consequently, Marx argued, the basic form of humanity was *not* the individual but the community. When Marx spoke of human nature, he was not referring to the human individual but to human society. Borrowing a term from Ludwig Feuerbach, Marx spoke of "species-being" or "species-life" as the basic element of human nature; we are human only in community or society, because it is only in a social setting that we can produce the objects of labor. Marx thus set himself sharply against the exaltation of the individual which characterized modern philosophy and political theory. Theories which stress the rights of the individual above all else were in clear conflict with Marx's social definition of human nature.

The Problem of Alienation

We have thus far described Marx's ideal view of humanity, i.e., the way human beings would act if everything were the way it ought to be. But things are not as they ought to be, and the distortion of authentic human being elicited a fervent anger in Marx. The philosophical conception of *praxis* sketched above was embedded in a forceful condemnation of the conditions which threatened the well-being of "species-life." Remember that according to Marx the goal of all thought was to change the world; thus Marx's interpretation of the human condition was part of a larger practical program to change those elements of modern life which threatened humanity. Keeping to his materialist orientation, Marx moved to analyze the *material conditions* which led to the *alienation* of humanity.

Marx's analysis focused on what he called the "political economy," i.e., those economic, political, and social structures characteristic of capitalist economies. He intended simply to reveal the internal contradictions inherent in the capitalist system. Marx contended that capitalism had disrupted the harmonious workings of human society in its natural state by creating the idea of *private property*. The private ownership of the products of labor arose only in a system motivated by greed in which the property owning class attempted to accumulate greater and greater wealth at the expense of the worker. He argued that the labor process was dehumanized and the worker's product became nothing more than a thing, a "commodity." But, said Marx, if human beings were what they produced, and products were seen to be things to be bought and sold, soon "the worker sinks to the level of a commodity and becomes indeed the most wretched of commodities."[5]

Marx described the progressive dehumanization of the labor process under the term *alienation*. Marx's discussion of alienation is powerful, both in its moral force and in the clarity of analysis. We need at this point to hear him speak in his own voice:

> All these consequences are contained in the definition that the worker is related to the *product of his labour* as to an *alien* object. For on this premise it is clear that the more the worker spends himself, the more powerful the alien objective world becomes which he creates over-against himself, the poorer he himself—his inner world—becomes, the less belongs to him as his own. . . . The worker puts his life into the object; but now his life no longer belongs to him but to the object. Hence, the greater this activity, the greater is the worker's lack of objects. Whatever the product of his labour is, he is not. Therefore the greater this product, the less is he himself. The *alienation* of the worker in his product means not only that his labour becomes an object, an *external* existence, but that it exists *outside* him, independently, as something alien to him, and that it becomes a power of its own confronting him; it means that the life which he has conferred on the object confronts him as something hostile and alien.[6]

Marx believed that the capitalist system thus subverted the essential aspect of human *praxis,* that the object produced by the laborer was the objectified form of his own species-life. When that object was taken from the worker and treated as a commodity to be bought and sold, it became impossible for the worker to see himself in that product. Thus the worker too began to treat the product of his labor as a dehumanized, hostile, and alien object. The effects of such alienation were far-reaching, said Marx. Not only was the worker alienated from the product of his work, he was also alienated from the activity of producing itself. The worker, in contrast to the artisan of our earlier example, could not "pour himself into" his product. Since he no longer saw himself in his product, he no longer gave himself to its production. Thus the essential human act of producing was distorted.

If that was the case, argued Marx, then alienation had to affect the very heart of human existence. Capitalism ultimately brought about a destruction of the "species-life." As a producer of commodities the worker lost all sense of the social dimension of human life. Working was no longer experienced as a communal activity done for the good of the whole society; it was rather an individual activity done for the sole purpose of sustaining individual life. Work lost its role as an essential human activity and became simply a means of maintaining physical life.

The end result of this breakdown of the communal character of work was the destruction of the very notion of "species-life" and the alienation of one human being from another. According to Marx, if the experience of engaging in common human activity in the workplace became increasingly foreign, then soon persons would view other human beings as essentially alien. Instead of seeing oneself in the other, the fellow human being would be seen as foreign, alien, and even hostile. Consequently, the whole of human relationships would be distorted through the alienating influence of capitalism.

Revolution: the Emancipation of Humanity

The clearest consequence of capitalist alienation was the creation of two radically different and antagonistic classes—"the property *owners* and the propertyless *workers.*" Much of Marx's "relentless criticism" was directed toward the class structure of the capitalist system. Marx felt that if philosophy was to change the world, it had to begin by understanding the conditions which made the world what it was: thus Marx's relentless criticism of class structure. Criticism was, however, never an end in itself but only a means to a practical end. The goal of criticism was "revolutionary practice." Marx was convinced that the dehumanizing contradictions of capitalism were so great that they could only be overcome through the destruction of capitalism itself. Once the capitalist class system was understood, it had to be used to bring about its own demise. That demise could only be accomplished through revolution. It is important to remember, however, that revolution for Marx was the means whereby *human emancipation* was accomplished. The goal of revolution was the destruction of the capitalist material conditions which caused human alienation. Only through the destruction of these conditions could the human species be freed for true nonalienating *praxis.*

The first step toward revolution was to allow capitalism to create a class of totally dispossessed persons: the proletariat.

> A class must be formed which has *radical chains,* a class in civil society which is not a class of civil society, a class which is the dissolution of all classes, a sphere of society which has a universal character because its sufferings are universal, and which does not claim a *particular redress* because the wrong which is done to it is not a *particular wrong* but *wrong in general.* A sphere, finally, which cannot emancipate itself without emancipating itself from all the other spheres of society, without, therefore, emancipating all these other spheres, which is, in short, a *total loss* of humanity and which can only redeem itself by a *total redemption* of humanity. This dissolution of society as a particular class, is the proletariat.[7]

The proletariat was the universally abused class whose plight could not be remedied without destroying the entire system which enslaved this class. The proletariat was the concrete representation of capitalism's dehumanizing contradictions. If the proletariat were emancipated, then the whole society would be simultaneously emancipated—though the emancipation had to take the form of violent revolution. But the goal of revolution was human emancipation through the liberation of the proletariat.

Again we have arrived at a key but difficult Marxian idea. How can the freeing of a particular class be the liberation of all humanity? Marx borrowed here an argument he learned from Hegel's *Phenomenology of Spirit* in the famous section entitled "Lordship and Bondage." A look at Hegel's argument might help us to understand Marx. Hegel analyzed the complex relationship of dependence between master and slave, saying the master sought to dominate the slave completely in order that the slave might learn what the master knew: that the master was fully independent and in control. In order for the master to be truly in control, he had to have the slave as the "other" in his relationship. But ironically it became clear to the master as he reflected on his situation that his project of full independence and control could not be achieved. He was "master" only because he was in relation to the "slave." He could not destroy the slave, for then he would no longer be master. But as long as he *needed* the slave, he could not be fully independent and in control. Thus, concluded Hegel, the project of total dominance or lordship was doomed to failure. The slave, on the other hand, could also recognize his own essential role in this relationship. If he were to see that he was not simply an instrument of the master, the slave could achieve the freedom of seeing his own human independence. Hegel determined that precisely as the master saw he was bound to the slave, the slave realized his independence from the master.

Marx, of course, was less interested in what the slave saw or understood than what he did. Once the slave (having been transformed into the social class of the proletariat) recognized his independence from the master, he had to act to destroy the conditions which enslaved them both. The master was as alienated as the slave as long as he accepted and supported the conditions which encouraged slavery. But the master, looking at the world through his alienation, saw no reason to change the dominant-subordinate relation. The master therefore could not be the agent for emancipation. Only the "class with radical chains" which was universally alienated and stood only to gain in the revolution could be the agent for effective change. But again the goal of revolution was the elimination of those structures which enslaved both slave and master. The goal was human emancipation.

> *Communism* as the *positive* transcendence of *private property*, or *human self-estrangement*, and therefore as the real *appropriation of the human essence* by and for man; communism therefore as the complete return of man to himself as a social (i.e., human) being.
>
> . . . The positive transcendence of *private property* as the appropriation of *human* life is, therefore, the positive transcendence of all alienation— that is to say, the return of man from religion, family, state, etc., to his *human,* i.e., *social* mode of existence.[8]

Marx drew back from describing the state to be reached following the emancipating revolution; he was content to say that it was a state in which alienation was overcome, humanity was returned to its true state, and social and communal existence was restored. Clearly this utopian vision in Marx exhibits strong religious qualities. The language of alienation, redemption, restoration, and transcendence has a long religious history prior to Marx's appropriation of it. And yet, as the final quotation indicates, Marx conceived of the postrevolutionary situation as one that no longer required religion. For Marx, human emancipation included emancipation from religion and religion's God. Emancipated humanity was atheistic humanity—a humanity without God.

Marx's humanistic vision of emancipation has had an enormous impact in modern society. His thought has provided a way to combine critical reflection and radical action on behalf of the poor and oppressed. Marxist thought has given many people concrete hope that liberation from economic oppression can be accomplished. Many Christians have been attracted to this bold expression of hope for the future. Yet the apparent atheism of Marx's position ought to trouble those Christians who see Marxism as an ally in the struggle for social justice. What is the relation between Marx's view of human nature and his atheism? How ought Christians respond to Marx's atheistic critique of religion? We turn to these questions in the next chapter.

3 Marx's Thought: Critique of Religion

by Ronald F. Thiemann

"Religion is the opium of the people." No single sentence Marx ever wrote is as well known to American Christians as this one. In light of the sentiment Marx expressed here, many Christians have assumed that conversation with antagonistic and atheistic Marxism is simply doomed to failure from the outset. How can a true conversation be carried on if one partner—the Marxist—denies the validity of the Christian's beliefs from the outset? That question is vitally important, and it may be that Marxism's antireligious polemic will be the stumbling block on which mutual understanding will flounder. But before that judgment can be made, we need to look more closely at Marx's critique of religion. What motivated his sharp condemnation of religion? What is the relationship between Marx's critique of religion and the humanistic anthropology we sketched in the preceding chapter? Is atheism an integral part of Marx's view of reality? These are some of the questions we will address in this chapter.

The first step toward a fuller understanding of Marx's view of religion is to place the brief sentence quoted above in its larger context.

> For Germany, the *criticism of religion* has been largely completed; and the criticism of religion is the premise of all criticism. . . . The basis of irreligious criticism is this: *man makes religion;* religion does not make man. . . . The struggle against religion is, therefore, indirectly a struggle against *that world* whose spiritual *aroma* is religion.

> *Religious* suffering is at the same time an *expression* of real suffering and a *protest* against real suffering. Religion is the sigh of the oppressed creature, the sentiment of a heartless world, and the soul of soulless conditions. It is the *opium* of the people.
>
> The abolition of religion as the *illusory* happiness of men, is a demand for their *real* happiness. The call to abandon their illusions about their condition is a *call to abandon a condition which requires illusions.*[1]

We need to examine this passage carefully in order to see the complexity of Marx's attitude toward religion.

"For Germany, the *criticism of religion* has been largely completed; and the criticism of religion is the premise of all criticism. . . ." Marx believed that Ludwig Feuerbach, a radical German philosopher of the mid-19th century, had developed the ultimate criticism of religion in his book *The Essence of Christianity.* Though Marx was often critical of Feuerbach (see *Theses on Feuerbach*), he accepted and presupposed Feuerbach's devastating challenge to Christian faith. Moreover, Marx was convinced that criticism of religion—and by that he meant destruction of belief in God—was the necessary first step toward the criticism of the economic ills of capitalism. Only when people ceased being dependent upon a divine being could they become responsible for their own actions and set about changing the alienating capitalist economy.

"The basis of irreligious criticism is this: *man makes religion;* religion does not make man." In this passage Marx summarized the key element of Feuerbach's attack on religion. Feuerbach argued quite simply that belief in God was an alienating illusion created by human beings in response to their own fears and desires. God was nothing other than a human creation, an illusory being who, believers imagined, could rescue them from the fears and disappointments which plague human life. Because human beings were finite, they constantly experienced themselves as limited, weak, and incomplete. Such experiences, particularly the prospect of death, created the fear of personal extinction and the desire for some rescue from this plight. The inevitable human response to this dilemma was to imagine that there was a being who was unlimited, all-powerful, and perfect who would come to their aid. People imagined this being as real and existing, gave him the name "God," and assigned him every good quality imaginable. Having created this God they now pretended that he was not the creation of imagination; rather, they believed that he was real and was the creator and redeemer. With that assumption the illusion was completed, fears were calmed, and they rested quietly in their dreams.

While such an illusion may be comforting, Feuerbach believed that it was finally destructive of human self-esteem. If God was the source of all that is powerful and good, then human beings had to be conceived as weak and lacking in good. If every positive quality was assigned to God, then we have only negative properties to assign to ourselves. Our exaltation of God becomes a denigration of humanity. Moreover, by conceiving of ourselves as dependent upon an all-powerful being we become passive and inactive, failing to take responsibility for our own lives. *Belief in God was in Feuerbach's eyes the key to all human alienation.* We have taken our own good qualities—love, compassion, trust—and assigned them to an alien being, a being who is "wholly other." Having projected our own good qualities onto God, we no longer recognize them as our own. They become the foreign and alien traits of a totally separate being. The comfort we receive from this illusion is false comfort, for it masks the deeper truth that belief in God alienates us from ourselves. Human beings cannot be rescued from alienation until that illusion is unmasked and destroyed. If belief in God is rejected, then human beings can regain their self-esteem and become responsible agents for change. Until this happens humanity will remain trapped in its alienating illusion called "God."

"The struggle against religion is, a struggle against *that world* whose spiritual *aroma* is religion." Feuerbach understood the criticism of religion to be the final step in overcoming human alienation. Marx, on the other hand, saw religious criticism as simply the essential *first* step in the battle against alienation. Religion was not the root cause but only a key symptom of human estrangement. The putrefying aroma rising from the decaying corpse of religion was but an indication that the entire world of which religion is a part was dying. Feuerbach's mistake was to assume that the death of religion would bring about human emancipation. Feuerbach had indeed performed the last rites over religion and lowered the corpse into its final resting place. But he failed to address the deeper malady of which religion was only one part—the problem of economic alienation. Once the religious corpse had been buried, then the final task of economic emancipation could begin.

"*Religious* suffering is at the same time an *expression* of real suffering and a *protest* against real suffering. Religion is the sign of the oppressed creature, the sentiment of a heartless world, and the soul of soulless conditions. It is the *opium* of the people." Marx's criticism of religion was sharp and unrelenting, but he did recognize a limited usefulness of religious belief. Though religion was an illusion, according to Marx, it was, nonetheless, an instructive illusion. Religious believers share with

Marxists the conviction that the world is flawed and distorted; creation is not what it was meant to be. Believers identify the distortion as sin and long for the release from sin which will come from redemption. That desire for deliverance is what Marx called "an expression of real suffering." Moreover, believers refuse to accept the flawed world as God's final will for his creation. God does not will that his creatures remain trapped in their state of sin. Consequently, religion opposes all those forces which bring about human misery and suffering, that is to say, religion is "a protest against real suffering."

Despite its real insight into the human condition, religion was finally, according to Marx, an opiate, because religion sought the solution to human suffering in the spiritual realm. Religion failed to see that both the problem and the solution to suffering lay in the material conditions of life. Those conditions could not be changed through worship and prayer but only through the human effort resulting in revolution. Religion sought happiness in God, in a blessed release to the other world, rather than working for happiness in this world through responsible human action. Because of its spiritual, otherworldly orientation, religion could never be more than "the sigh of the oppressed creature"; it could never become a resource for overcoming oppression. For that reason it would always remain "the opium of the people."

"The abolition of religion as the *illusory* happiness of men, is a demand for their *real* happiness. The call to abandon their illusions about their condition is a *call to abandon a condition which requires illusions.*" Marx did not believe that socialists should actively oppose religion or seek to destroy it. Rather he was convinced that once the revolution was accomplished the need for religion would vanish, and religion would simply disappear. Religion, according to Marx, was an illusory way of dealing with human alienation. As long as economic alienation persisted, religion would remain a pervasive, though deeply flawed, response to suffering. Religion's mistake was that it offered spiritual balm for a material wound. Religion treated only the symptoms of the disease (spiritual distress) and not the disease itself (economic injustice). Revolutionary socialism struck at the disease, and when the disease was cured the symptoms would vanish, along with the need for false cures.

This medical analogy provides a useful way of explaining Marx's final attitude toward religion: The pain of cancer is often so great that the patient must be given a narcotic like opium to provide temporary relief from suffering. The narcotic, however, treats only the symptom of pain; it leaves the cancerous tumor untouched. Only radical surgery to remove the cancer can provide the ultimate cure. If the surgery is successful then pain will subside of its own accord, and all temporary narcotics will be unnecessary. Marxist thought would say that the revolution of the proletariat will accomplish the radical surgery on the cancerous material conditions of modern society. When that cancer is removed, suffering will be eliminated, and the need for the opiate relief of religious illusion will be eliminated as well.

Marx was convinced that the revolution would usher in an age in which human beings would take full responsibility for their actions, achieve complete maturity and autonomy, and fashion a just and equitable society. He believed that when this final stage was reached, human beings would recognize that the only reality is human reality, i.e., the social and communal reality of species-life. Then human beings would give full and free expression to their active laboring lives without the accompanying alienation caused by capitalism. The human species would finally achieve the perfect expression of *praxis* for which it was intended. *Praxis* would become the "evident and incontrovertible proof of (human) *self-creation.*"[2] True *praxis* would bring about the recognition that human beings are masters of their own destinies—that they are self-creators. When emancipated *praxis* became a reality, the creating and sustaining God of religion would simply wither away.

The Christian Response

How should Christians respond to the challenge represented by Marx's thought? In large part the remaining chapters of this book will attempt to address that question. At this point it seems appropriate simply to highlight some of the issues which Marx's thought raises for Christians.

Some aspects of Marx's thinking appear congenial to Christian belief. Marx's categories of alienation and emancipation bear a strong resemblance to the Christian ideas of sin and redemption. The hopeful future-directed quality of his thought sounds familiar to Christians nurtured on the hope of the gospel. Yet despite these formal similarities, Marx interpreted his categories in ways Christians find puzzling or even offensive. The thoroughgoing materialist orientation of Marx's thinking serves as a particular barrier to a sympathetic Christian interpretation of Marx. Marx's definition of alienation in economic or material terms sounds both narrow and naive to Christian ears. Can alienation be reduced to the economic conditions which determine the process of production? Is every form of human alienation reducible to economic categories? Can every act of human injustice, exploitation, and hatred be explained by reference to people's economic situation? Christians will naturally want to broaden both the symptoms and causes of alienation beyond the material. Particularly Christians will be anxious to locate alienation in the human desire to turn away from God and humanity in an act of prideful rebellion. Is the Marxist category of alienation sufficiently broad to include some traditional Christian notion of sin? The issue of materialism is clearly one which needs deeper examination in the conversation between Christians and Marxists.

On the other hand Marx's materialism raises an important challenge to Christian belief. If Marx was one-sidedly materialistic, Christianity has traditionally been one-sidedly spiritualistic. Despite the centrality of the doctrine of the incarnation, Christian theology has only rarely stressed the importance of the sensuous and material. Christian theology should be led by its own doctrines of creation and incarnation to offer a theological interpretation of the material conditions of human life. The predominant spiritual side of the Christian faith has made it difficult to incorporate material and economic ideas into our notions of human nature, sin, redemption, and sanctification. The encounter with Marx may serve as the occasion for Christians to rediscover the material side of God's creation—to make deeper sense of God's formation of human beings from the dust of the ground, of God's entrance into the material of human flesh in Jesus Christ. If Christians are to criticize Marx for his apparent one-sidedness, we need also to hear his criticism of a too narrow Christian spiritualism which ignores the material economic conditions of human existence.

Marx's stress on action also raises interesting issues. Christians will rightly resist the reduction of all thought to economic criticism. Theology as a form of Christian thinking must have an independence from economic analysis. Yet Marx serves as a helpful reminder that Christian theology ultimately has a practical goal. Theology is designed to serve the *practice of Christian faith*. While faith has a side we rightly call spiritual, Christian practice is also oriented toward the material. Dialogue with Marxism can help renew the Christian commitment to social and economic justice. While the goal and rationale for Christian action must be the gospel of Jesus Christ, continuing study of Marxism might serve as an occasion for uniting more clearly the spiritual and material dimensions of Christian thought and practice.

Marx's view of humanity as essentially social raises another important challenge to Christians. The Protestant tradition in particular has been highly individualistic in its interpretation of human nature. Luther's understanding of justification as dependent solely on the faith of the believer gives a strong individualistic cast to Protestant theology. One is not saved by the institutional structure of the church, nor by the intercession of the saints, but solely through faith in the redemption accomplished in Jesus Christ. The great Protestant theologians—Luther, Calvin, Schleiermacher, Kierkegaard, Niebuhr, and many others—have defined the essential form of humanity as the individual. But such positions have been notoriously hard pressed to give a sufficient account of the importance of Christian community. All too often Christian community is seen to be little more than a voluntary collection of individual believers. But is such a view sufficient to the centrality that the concepts of "kingdom of God" and "body of Christ"—communal concepts—have in the New Testament? Might the encounter with Marx help Christians to see new possibilities in our own tradition for a fuller social and communal understanding of Christian existence? Such an emphasis on community seems especially important at a time when all forms of communal life are under attack by the modern cult of the individual.

Christians can learn much from a careful study of Marxism but surely the greatest barrier to mutual affirmation lies in the atheism of Marx's thought. Some interpreters of Marx have argued that Marx's atheism was borrowed from Feuerbach and is easily detached from the rest of his thought. But if the interpretation offered in these two chapters is correct, Marx's atheism is not a casual afterthought but an essential component of his view of *praxis*. For Marx, human beings were truly free only when they were fully responsible for their own actions. Emancipation—the overcoming of alienation—was achieved when humanity depended on nothing else but itself, when it acknowledged itself as its own creator. Emancipation for Marx was nothing less than the assertion of *human self-creation*. Any claim to dependency upon God for life, sustenance, and redemption was a step away from emancipation toward the chains of alienation. At the deepest level Marx's commitment to *praxis* and the Christian commitment to dependence upon the grace of God appear incompatible.

This apparent incompatibility may limit the extent of agreement which can be reached between Christians and Marxists. It may also limit the usefulness of Marxist analysis for Christian social action. But the conflict should not foreclose conversation between these two influential traditions. Each has much to learn from the other. Both communities continue to grow and develop, and the movement of history may raise new possibilities for dialogue. As you will read in a later chapter, Western Marxists have radically redefined some of Marx's own concepts in light of new historical reality. While Marxists at this point seem no more disposed to deny the atheism of *praxis* than Christians are to deny belief in God, that fact should not bring the conversation to a halt. On the question of *praxis* and God, the conversation may consist of nothing more than a mutually contradictory confession of faith. But such a conflicting witness is surely preferable to the antagonism born of ignorance. The future of such conversation and witness will be committed by the Marxist to the inexorable movement of the material forces of history and by the Christian to the providential grace of God.

4 Marx's Thought: Materialistic Understanding of History

by Wayne C. Stumme

Since, however, for socialist man, the *whole of what is called world history* is nothing but the creation of man by human labor, and the emergence of nature for man, he, therefore, has the evident and irrefutable proof of his *self-creation,* of his own *origins.*[1]

Karl Marx

In the 11th of his famous *Theses on Feuerbach,* Karl Marx wrote, "The philosophers have only *interpreted* the world, in various ways; the point, however, is to *change* it."[2] Yet what is to be changed must also be understood and interpreted, and that is what Marx attempted to do. His writings exhibit a unique fusion of the critical detachment of a historian and the passionate commitment of a revolutionary. For him the study of history became a weapon in the struggle for a radically different society.

Marx's method and conclusions came to be known as *historical materialism.* Within that conceptual framework he set forth a penetrating analysis of emerging industrial capitalism; he presented a comprehensive and provocative philosophy of history; and he offered the working class a revolutionary program. Marx was convinced that the key to under-standing social change was to be found in the way that humans produced their common life. History was the story of that process of social and material development, a process charged with the tension between what was and what was coming to be. The outcome of this historical move-ment, Marx declared, was a profound and humanizing transformation of society. History was to be viewed from a perspective of hope.

Humanity "Makes" History

Marx had already rejected prevailing views of history by the time he put forward his revolutionary alternative. History for him was not the arena in which powerful ideals contended, nor was it the record of the activity of influential persons. Even earlier he had repudiated the belief that history was guided by the divine will and subject to divine inter-vention.

Marx approached history as the concrete and observable activity of humans. His starting point was clear:

> We must begin by stating the first premise of all human existence and therefore, of all human history, the premise, namely, that men must be in a position to live in order to "make history". . . . The first historical act is thus the production of the means to satisfy these needs, the pro-duction of material life itself.[1]

History, then, was the account of what people did together in order to live. To be human was to be a social creature, to have relations with others for the sake of life itself. Those relations, Marx carefully noted, would vary greatly, and he distinguished between what he called Asiatic, ancient, feudal, and modern bourgeois societies. He pointed out that primitive societies, for example, had a "mode of production" different from that characteristic of feudalism, and the medieval pattern itself was supplanted by the "bourgeois" or capitalist manner of "producing the means of subsistence." What was common to all, he asserted, was that the relations of individuals to one another changed as the way they "produced their life" through work and exchange developed.

Social existence, therefore, always had an economic "base." This was fundamental for Marx's understanding of history.

> Thus it is quite obvious from the start that there exists a materialistic connection of men with one another, which is determined by their needs and their mode of production, and which is as old as men themselves.

> This connection is ever taking on new forms, and thus presents a "history" independently of the existence of any political or religious nonsense which would especially hold men together.[4]

That "materialistic connection," or "base," was also decisive in shaping the laws, customs, culture, and religion of a society. These latter, said Marx, formed the social "superstructure," which in turn reflected the actual relations of persons engaged in the essential economic activity. Thus their "consciousness," or common way of looking at life, was an accurate expression of the way that they dealt with one another as they produced what was required for life. Ideas and beliefs, Marx contended, were not independent of society and did not determine its direction.

How did Marx account for the conflict which had always accompanied the association of individuals with one another? His answer provides an important clue to his understanding of history. "The history of all hitherto existing society," said Marx in a famous passage from the *Communist Manifesto,* "is the history of class struggles."[5] He was not describing how people in a given society felt about their condition but how certain "objective factors" brought about social change. He summarized it in these words:

> At a certain stage of their development, the material productive forces of society come into conflict with the existing relations of production, or—which is but a legal expression for the same thing—with the property relations within which they have been at work hitherto. From forms of development of the productive forces, these relations turn into their fetters. Then begins an epoch of social revolution.[6]

Marx traced the emergence of the conflict to what he termed the "division of labor," that economic arrangement in which different persons carried out different and limited tasks in the production process. Recognizing that the division of labor was necessary if human productive activity was to satisfy growing human needs, he also predicted its destructive results. Marx believed that it led directly to the unequal and unfair distribution of what labor had produced cooperatively. That economic inequality was unmistakably expressed in the institution of "private property."

What Marx meant by private property was ownership by individuals of the means of production, namely land, raw materials, machinery, and capital. That was a social "contradiction," Marx held, an unresolved conflict arising from the unequal relations of those engaged in the production of goods. Private property, furthermore, led to the appearance of classes, social and economic groups marked off from one another by their roles in the productive process and by the extent of their ownership of what was produced.

Class hostility would grow irresistibly, Marx said, as each group would find its self-interest increasingly threatened. At the same time, the great mass of workers would sink into even greater destitution, while the owners of the means of production would increase both their wealth and power. Class struggle was inevitable, Marx concluded, and reflected the exploitative conditions imposed upon the workers in the productive process itself.

The Era of Bourgeois Society

What Marx had pictured was not a theoretical construction. He was describing the "bourgeois mode of production," the amazing phenomenon of industrial capitalism which transformed completely the societies of 19th-century Europe and North America. Acknowledging its successes, he termed it "the most developed and the most complex historic organization of production."[7] He viewed industrial capitalism as a necessary stage through which human history had to pass, and he recognized that it had attained the highest level of social production yet known. Marx's lifelong concern was to understand how this new economic and social order functioned, to describe where it was going, and to anticipate its eventual overthrow.

Yet bourgeois society was able to produce a greater amount of what humans needed for life than had any of its predecessors. Why seek to overthrow a system which apparently held so much promise? Marx was in no doubt about the answer. More than most of his contemporaries, he was aware of the desperate poverty of the industrial working classes. In addition to the hazardous working conditions in many factories, the new economic order failed to share beyond the level of bare subsistence its wealth with those who produced it. As Marx shrewdly observed, "The structure of distribution is completely determined by the structure of production."[8] Since the latter was securely controlled by the rising bourgeois, or owners' class, the workers could expect little improvement in their miserable situation.

In addition, governments tended to exhibit in their legal structure and administration the favored position of the property owning classes, and offered the impoverished and powerless workers little protection or legal recourse. Marx, therefore, did not call for the reform of a system which he judged fundamentally unjust, but for radical political action, for "liberation." As he wrote:

> . . . it is only possible to achieve real liberation in the real world and by employing real means . . . and that, in general, people cannot be liberated as long as they are unable to obtain food and drink, housing and clothing in adequate quality and quantity. "Liberation" is a historical and not a mental act, and it is brought about by historical conditions.[9]

Here was the liberation which so completely occupied Marx: the political and economic deliverance of the exploited working classes in 19th-century industrial society.

Marx was even more specific in his understanding of the oppressiveness of capitalist society. He cited a number of factors, each of which was connected with the actual social relations which were typical of the bourgeois mode of production.

"Capital," declared Marx, "is the all-dominating power of bourgeois society."[10] This critical factor determined the nature of the society and the relationships of persons within it. Because modern capital represented "pure private property, which has cast off all semblance of a communal institution,"[11] it is not inhibited from shaping the communal expression of society—the state—to its own ends. As Marx put it, "The executive of the modern State is but a committee for managing the common affairs of the whole bourgeoisie."[12] Those "common affairs" were directed toward the accumulation of capital. Marx described that accumulation as occuring through rents, usury, mercantile profits, colonial exploitation, and the wealth extracted from unpaid labor. He saw that capital, contrary to the claims made for it ("money makes money"), was unproductive apart from the labor of human beings.

That latter point was made with striking clarity in the *Communist Manifesto:*

> The essential condition for the existence, and for the sway of the bourgeois class, is the formation and augmentation of capital; the condition for capital is wage-labor. Wage-labor rests exclusively on competition between the laborers.[13]

Wage-labor, as described by Marx, was the "living labor" of persons compelled to sell their "labor power" in order to live. While workers exchanged their labor for wages, this process, contrary to appearances, was not a fair exchange. For through the wage system, the owners of the means of production "appropriated" without recompense a portion of the wealth created by the workers. Marx depicted this appropriation in his theory of "surplus value." He pointed out that the wealth created by human labor was only partially returned in the form of wages. The workers received what was necessary for their survival and the entrepreneurs kept the remainder for themselves. From the standpoint of the workers, whose labor had produced wealth in the form of products, this process was exploitation or, as an earlier socialist had put it, theft.

Marx's critique of bourgeois society went beyond the analysis of wage labor and the accumulation of capital. He pointed out that just as the products of wage-labor became "commodities"—things having use value and available to others through exchange—so the workers themselves increasingly were dealt with as impersonal commodities. Within the entirety of bourgeois society the workers were "thus robbed of all real life-content" and became "abstract individuals,"[14] totally "alienated." Industrial capitalism had become a dehumanizing force for the great majority of those who produced its wealth.

Where would all of this lead? Marx thundered his reply:

> The bourgeois relations of production are the last antagonistic form of the social process of production—antagonistic not in the sense of individual antagonism, but of one arising from the social conditions of life of the individuals; at the same time the productive forces developing in the womb of bourgeois society create the material conditions for the solution of that antagonism.[15]

Such "antagonism" had specific content. The class of the propertyless workers—the proletariat—stood in growing opposition to the class of property owners—the bourgeoise. Marx held that the self-interest of these two classes was in irreconcilable opposition. Since "the structure of distribution is completely determined by the structure of production,"[16] no solution in terms of a more equitable sharing of socially produced wealth was possible. The "forms of development" of bourgeois society finally had become the "fetters" of the working masses; the historically progressive had become the historically obsolete. History, as viewed by Marx, was an inexorable movement, advancing through the debris of outmoded social systems and destined to overcome existing social contradictions. The transformative force of history, born "in the womb of bourgeois society," was the proletariat.

History and Human Consciousness

Marx concluded that the emergence of capitalism and its eventual dissolution were phenomena dictated by the laws of historical development. He was not alone in thinking of human progress in these terms. The emergence of a new mode of production and its accompanying society, the increasing "contradictions" experienced in this development, and the eventual supersession of the existing society by a superior form of social organization: this pattern reveals the influence of the philosopher Hegel upon Marx.

If history, however, was the interplay of dynamic and conflict-ridden forces, what could be said about the significance of human awareness and action? It would be incorrect to interpret Marx as a mechanistic determinist, denigrating the human contribution to the resolution of historical problems. At the same time, he recognized the limits within which persons had to work.

> Men make their own history, but they do not make it just as they please; they do not make it under circumstances chosen by themselves, but under circumstances directly encountered, given and transmitted from the past.[17]

"Past circumstances" were a decisive factor in the formation and expression of human consciousness, that unique awareness which precedes and accompanies all human activity. As was noted earlier, Marx considered consciousness and language to be social products.

> Language, like consciousness, only arises from the need, the necessity, of intercourse with other men. . . . Consciousness is, therefore, from the very beginning a social product, and remains so for as long as men exist at all.[18]

What Marx had said about social production in general could be applied equally well to his view of the creation of human self-awareness, namely, that "the *entire so-called history of the world* is nothing but the begetting of man through human labor."[19] Human productive activity was the key to understanding consciousness, not ideas, since "life is not determined by consciousness, but consciousness by life."[20]

Consciousness, however, was not a neutral phenomenon. Marx insisted that consciousness was formed in accordance with the way that persons organized their necessary productive activity. Different forms of consciousness—such as religion, philosophy, ethics, law, and art—had as their determining "basis" the "real process of production." These forms were "theoretical products," according to Marx, and could only be depicted with accuracy when the economic "base" and the social "superstructure" were seen in their reciprocal relationship.[21] The nature of that relationship continues to be debated by contemporary adherents of Marxism.

In particular, Marx focused on the problem of consciousness in a bourgeois society. He had no illusions about what had happened.

> The ideas of the ruling class are in every epoch the ruling ideas: i.e., the class which is the ruling *material* force of society, is at the same time its ruling *intellectual* force. . . . The ruling ideas are nothing more than the ideal expression of the dominant material relationships, the dominant material relationships grasped as ideas; hence of the relationships which make the one class the ruling class, therefore, the ideas of its dominance.[22]

The class-generated "ideas of its dominance" are what Marx means by "ideology." Taken together, these ideas function to maintain the existing privileges of wealth and power, that is, in effect, to perpetuate human inequality and oppression. An ideology subordinates questions of "truth" and "right" to the vital interests of the ruling group. Marx did not exempt religion from his harsh criticism, for he held that it was a form of ideology—an "inverted world consciousness"—which provided "the general basis of consolation and justification" for bourgeois society.[23] No variety of idealism, he contended, should be allowed to mask the ideological distortion of human consciousness under industrial capitalism. "In one word, it creates a world after its own image."[24] It was that world, Marx believed, that had enslaved the mind as it had fettered the body. What then was to be done?

The Epoch of Class Struggle . . . and Beyond

How can the world not only be interpreted but changed? How can history overcome the social contradictions inherent in the confrontation of powerful wealth with powerless poverty? What is the "solution of that antagonism"? How can the false, enslaving consciousness of persons in bourgeois society be abolished? How can the productive forces of a society come to serve the needs of all individuals? The answer of Marx can be summed up in a single word: *revolution!*

History itself had prepared the agent of liberation, Marx declared, and that agent was the proletariat. Created entirely by capitalist exploitation of labor, this class represented "a sphere of society which has a universal character because its sufferings are universal."[25]

> A class is called forth which has to bear all the burdens of society without enjoying its advantages, which, ousted from society, is forced into the

> most decided antagonism to all other classes; a class which forms the
> majority of all members of society, and from which emanates the con-
> sciousness of the necessity of a fundamental revolution, the communist
> consciousness.[26]

Made up of the victims of industrial capitalist society, the proletariat
had a historic vocation. Through its revolutionary activity, this class
would mediate the thoroughgoing transformation of human history.

"The material conditions for the solution of that antagonism" had
been created.[27] The proletariat had come into existence, and was conscious of its vocation to class struggle and, ultimately, revolutionary
practice. As Marx said,

> This revolution is necessary not only because the *ruling* class cannot be
> overthrown in any other way, but also because the class *overthrowing* it
> can only in a revolution succeed in ridding itself of all the muck of ages
> and become fitted to found society anew.[28]

Here can be seen something of the appeal to oppressed people of Marx's
comprehensive vision of history. He called for a new society *and* a new
human being, both created through the purified consciousness and revolutionary action of the masses (praxis). Such a profound alteration of
corporate and individual life could only occur through a "practical
movement, a revolution," for " 'liberation' is a historical and not a
mental act."[29]

The revolutionary commitment of Marx translated itself into specific
aims: "formation of the proletariat into a class, overthrow of the bourgeois supremacy, conquest of political power by the proletariat."[30] He
did not believe that revolution always required violence, and he anticipated that in certain countries (including the United States) radical social
change could take place through the political activity of the workers.
Whatever the means, the immediate goal remained constant: the proletariat must "appropriate" the means of production, and these "must
be made subject to each individual, and property to all. . . . With the
appropriation of the total productive forces through united individuals,
private property comes to an end."[31]

What would be the consequences of a successful revolution? Marx's
vision of the future was grounded in the conviction that "the emancipation of the workers contains universal human emancipation."[32] What,
more specifically, would that mean? The "division of labor" which
had contributed to the alienation of the workers would no longer char-
acterize productive life. In an idyllic picture of the coming communist

society, Marx suggested that "nobody has one exclusive sphere of activity but each can become accomplished in any branch he wishes; society regulates the general production and thus makes it possible for me to do one thing today and another tomorrow."[33]

Furthermore, the antagonistic relationship of competing classes would be overcome, because the proletarian revolution "abolishes the rule of all classes with the classes themselves" since the proletariat is "a class which no longer counts as a class in society, is not recognized as a class, and is in itself the dissolution of all classes, nationalities, etc., within present society."[34] He summarized his hope for the coming human community in these striking words from the *Manifesto:*

> In place of the old bourgeois society, with its classes and class antagonisms, we shall have an association, in which the free development of each is the condition for the free development of all.[35]

What would be the role of the state in this communist future? Marx had identified it as "the organized power of one class for oppressing another,"[36] and Engels later wrote of its "withering away" in a society where classes no longer existed. At most, Marx believed, the state would be servant and not master.

> As soon as the goal of the proletariat movement, the abolition of classes, shall have been reached, the power of the State, whose function it is to keep the great majority of producers beneath the yoke of a small minority of exploiters, will disappear and governmental functions will be transformed into simple administrative functions.[37]

There would still be need, however, for the victorious proletariat to exercise political power in the period following the revolution. Thus the State would continue in the interim before the full achievement of communist society, but in a different form. As Marx wrote:

> Between capitalist and communist society lies the period of the revolutionary transformation of the one into the other. There corresponds to this also a political transition period in which the State can be nothing but the *revolutionary dictatorship of the proletariat.*[38]

Marx said little about the final outcome of the revolutionary transformation of society. In a well-known passage from his major work, *Capital,* he did speculate about the movement of humanity from the "realm of necessity" to the "realm of freedom."

> Freedom in this field can only consist in socialized man, the associated producers, rationally regulating their interchange with Nature, bringing it under their common control, instead of being ruled by it as by the blind forces of Nature; and achieving this with the least expenditure of energy and under conditions most favorable to, and worthy of, their human nature. But it nonetheless remains a realm of necessity. Beyond it begins the development of human energy which is an end in itself, the true realm of freedom, which, however, can blossom forth only with the realm of necessity as its basis.[39]

This was the revolutionary vision of Marx. The success of the proletariat would bring "the prehistory of human society to a close,"[40] for *"all those conditions* in which man is an abased, enslaved, abandoned and contemptible being"[41] would have been overthrown. At that point, Marx believed, humanity would begin its true and fulfilling history.

Concluding Reflections

This chapter has summarized the leading ideas in Karl Marx's understanding of history. His extensive writings discuss historical materialism in far greater depth and detail, and this brief sketch has had to omit a number of his significant insights. No attempt was made to describe the development and application of his views by later Marxists. Neither have criticisms of the materialist understanding of history by Marxists and non-Marxists been included in this summary.

It should be noted that his theories of historical change have stimulated vigorous response by economists, historians, sociologists, and philosophers. Some aspects of his thought, developed in the context of 19th-century Europe, may seem less relevant in a world divided between preindustrial societies and nations moving into the "postindustrial" age of advanced technology. It is more than likely, however, that Marx would have responded to these new challenges as he did to those of his own time. Perhaps to a greater extent than the majority of his modern followers, he was willing critically to revise his work as new evidence presented itself.

Marx's materialist understanding of history poses particular questions for Christians. Our response can lead to a more profound appreciation of the Christian tradition as it engages the crucial issues of our time. At the same time, we may prepare ourselves for the necessary dialogue with men and women influenced by the thought of Marx and his successors. Following is a brief list of issues which Marx's concept of history raises for Christians.

Social structures and the struggle for justice. Marx has set forth one way of understanding how social institutions which serve the interests of particular classes can have dehumanizing consequences. Christians, in their biblically-grounded concern for social justice, must also seek critically to understand those present economic and political systems which exploit rather than serve people. Such understanding is essential for Christians if they are to participate in the shaping of more humane, just, and free social structures.

The critique of religion. Christians who have heard Marx's attack upon religion as "the perverted consciousness of a perverted society" will need to acknowledge the persistent temptation to cultural accommodation by the church. When theology becomes ideology and religious practices a form of justification for the status quo, the integrity and the freedom of the gospel are seriously threatened.

The responsibility of the human. Marx held that "man is the highest being for man" and that the goal of history was the "new human being," understood in both a collective and individual sense. We need to ask to what extent this view of the human is a *common* conviction of our contemporaries, Marxist and non-Marxist. How can the Christian message, which itself holds forth hope for a redeemed humanity, speak to this modern consciousness? In addition to what Christians would say about persistent human sinfulness, what can we say *positively* about the significance of human activity directed toward a better human future?

The failure of the human. Given the persuasiveness of Marx's understanding of alienation in modern industrial society, how can that view be deepened and corrected through critical encounter with the Christian doctrine of human sinfulness? How is the persistence of the tragic (e.g., sin) to be dealt with in any society which we may conceive, classless or otherwise? What is the meaning of grace and forgiveness in situations where the tragic assumes social proportions?

The agent of social renewal. Marx saw the proletariat—exploited, debased, and enslaved—as the class whose revolutionary action would bring about a more humane, egalitarian, just, and free future. That future would arrive through the combination of impersonal historical forces and enlightened human activity. For Marx the activity, and thus the reality, of God was totally excluded. How can Christians, in their inescapable commitment to the poor, avoid the political fanaticism which frequently accompanies such secular "messianism"? How can Christians witness in situations of social injustice and conflict to the transforming and "liberating" activity of *God* in history? How are we to understand and follow *God's* Messiah, Jesus, in the social conflicts of our day?

These are issues raised for Christians by Marx's understanding of history. They continue to occupy us as we seek in our time to live in "the obedience of faith" and with "love for the neighbor."

Historical Development
of Marxism

5 Socialism and Communism in the Industrial Nations

by Russell B. Norris Jr.

The Diversity of Marxism

In the 100 years since his death, the writings of Karl Marx have had a profound impact on the human race. There is virtually no place on earth where Marx's influence has not been felt. His shadow has fallen across the political development of many nations, not only in Eastern Europe but in Asia, Africa, Latin America, and the Middle East. This chapter will trace the growth of that influence during this century and will attempt to gauge its effect on the modern world.

Before beginning, it is necessary to clarify what is meant by the term *Marxist*. The names *Marxist, socialist*, and *communist* often are used interchangeably, not only in the West but within the Marxist camp itself. In fact, these terms have quite different meanings, and to confuse them will make it difficult to understand the differences among those who trace their thought and practice to Karl Marx.

In the broadest sense, socialism can be described as "a movement centered on uncompromising opposition to capitalism, giving preeminence to the economic aspect of life, convinced that the end of capitalism will usher in an era of permanent prosperity, peace and progress; aimed at achieving an egalitarian and brotherly society through the abolition of most or all individual ownership of property; strengthened by the certainty of possessing the truth and the key to happiness for all.''[1] From the beginning, however, these broad principles have taken different shapes in different contexts. From a critical revision of these convictions—in some cases bordering on outright rejection—came contemporary democratic socialism. From a dogmatic application of these same beliefs came Marxist-Leninism and other varieties of authoritarian socialism. For purposes of simplification, the term *Communist* is applied to the latter. The appellation *Marxist,* however, has been adopted by many socialist and revolutionary movements which have little to do with the kind of Marxism found in the Soviet Union and Eastern Europe.

This multifaceted development of Marxism is characteristic of the 20th century. When Karl Marx and Friedrich Engels began their long collaboration in the mid-19th century, they confronted the many forms of socialism which had sprung up in the wake of the Industrial Revolution.[2] The views of these two men, however, rapidly became decisive in socialist circles outside of the English-speaking world. More and more, socialists turned to them for a clear and cogent system of ideas which interpreted the past, explained the present, and offered guidelines for the future.

The Development of Marxism-Leninism

The movement had only a few thousand adherents in the late 1870s, but by the early 20th century the followers of Marx and Engels had become a powerful political force. They were active in Russia after the granting of a constitution in 1905, and they were even stronger in pre-World War Germany and France. In November 1917, the Bolsheviks (numerically the smallest of the Russian socialist groupings) seized power and precipitated a crisis in the socialist movement, polarizing the Russian Left. Bolshevism came to be the common term for revolutionary Russian Marxism, which later developed into what is known as Marxist-Leninism or, in political terms, communism.[3]

While bolshevism owed much of its character to its Russian origins, its primary shape was determined by its leader for two decades, Vladimir Ilyich Ulyanov, better known as Lenin. He was a brilliant theoretician and a ruthless politician. Whatever he might have thought about the deterministic elements in Marx's thought, Lenin acted in practice as though the human will could change the course of history. He stressed the importance of violence in the struggle for a socialist society, and he modified Marx's notion of the dictatorship of the proletariat by substituting the rule of the party on behalf of the workers. He totally rejected compromise (except where it was expedient), and his total devotion to the socialist cause meant a disavowal of ethical standards in favor of the principle that "the end justifies the means."

Lenin had assumed leadership of the Bolsheviks in 1903, only five years after the party had been secretly organized. His determination and strong leadership compensated for the party's lack of members, and the Bolsheviks became a catalyst of the revolution. What began with a few Russian exiles and then attracted thousands of intellectuals and workers is today a movement claiming the allegiance of tens of millions throughout the world.

After Lenin's death, his chief lieutenants—Trotsky, Zinoviev, Bukharin, and Stalin—competed for the leadership of the movement. By 1927 Stalin had achieved governmental control, and for the next quarter of a century was the undisputed leader of the Soviet Union and world communism. His major contributions to the Soviet version of Marxism included the application of Lenin's principles to economic organization, the weeding out of political dissidents, and the support of Communists who seized power in Eastern Europe and the Far East.

Many socialists were repelled by the cruelty of the 1918-1921 Red Terror, the programs of Soviet collectivization in the 1930s, the Stalinist purges of 1936-1938, the liquidation or deportation of minorities, the suppression of individual freedoms, and the armed occupation of foreign territories. The worst offenses of the czars appeared minor compared to the excesses of the new Soviet regime. Despite this criticism of Bolshevik actions on the part of socialists, the number of non-Communist revolutionaries declined steadily during the 1920s and 1930s and remained a significant force only in Spain. By 1939 Marxist-Leninism had become a worldwide movement under the leadership of the Soviet Union.

Communism In the Postwar Era

Following World War II, the monolithic character of communism was shaken by internal developments within the Soviet Union as well as by the growing independence of a few powerful non-Soviet Marxist leaders. As early as 1948 Stalin had been defied by the Yugoslav Communist leader, Josip Broz-Tito, who controlled his own military forces and counted on some support from the United States in the event of a Russian attack.

Stalin's death in 1953 was followed by a power struggle among the Soviet party hierarchy. The conflict did not result in significant institutional changes in the Soviet system although it did permit some alteration in economic policies and foreign relations. The authority of the

Soviets in the world socialist movement was weakened. Disturbances in East Germany, Poland, and Hungary (and later Czechoslovakia) were suppressed, but more successful was the movement away from Soviet hegemony of the Yugoslavs, the Albanians, and the Rumanians, and most notably, the Chinese. Yugoslav and Chinese Communists led their own armed forces; Albanians were geographically isolated from other Communist nations; Rumanian leaders played on the difference within the Soviet leadership and among the rulers of restive Communist countries. These factors gave them an autonomy which other Marxist nations did not enjoy and permitted the development of distinctive currents of Marxist thought, variously labeled "revisionist" and "dogmatist" by their opponents.

The postwar period has resulted in striking changes in some Eastern European Marxist states, including a movement away from the earlier internationalism and a growing conviction that socialism should reflect the national situation and culture. One gauge of such a development can be found in the relationships of the various Communist parties and the churches. In some instances this relationship has issued in growing cooperation and dialogue.[4]

In the years immediately following World War II, almost all Eastern European governments established a "postrevolutionary" policy designed to lead to the obliteration of the churches or at least the severe restriction of their activities. This was accompanied by an aggressive program of antireligious propaganda. Every one of these regimes, with the possible exception of the German Democratic Republic and Poland, went through this phase for a longer or shorter time, only to decide that it was not a workable long-range policy. Today only Albania aggressively pursues the elimination of all organized religion, and in 1967 made the claim to be the world's first totally atheistic country. Reports by outside observers confirm that Albania has succeeded in destroying its churches and mosques.[5]

In three other nations—the Soviet Union, Bulgaria, and Rumania—the churches and the state have achieved only limited forms of cooperation. An uneasy truce continues in the Soviet Union, where the leader of the propaganda section of the Party has declared that the disappearance of religion is the *sine qua non* for the building up of socialism. The limited attempts of some Russian Orthodox leaders to be supportive of the government are received with some ambivalence.

Christians in Bulgaria suffered a period of intense persecution from 1948 into the middle 1950s. During this time the government succeeded in "domesticating" the churches. Today the churches are officially cooperative in exchange for a narrowly construed "freedom" to worship.

The Communist party of Rumania seems to have had more need for the cooperation of Christians than its Soviet or Bulgarian counterparts. Until the 1960s Rumania was a docile satellite of the Soviet Union, but since then it has undertaken a more "maverick" policy which is intended to achieve greater national independence. Maintaining a strict and authoritarian rule domestically, the government seeks to rally the people to the support of Rumanian nationalism. The Orthodox church is viewed as a body which can promote internal cohesion, and as a result the Rumanian churches enjoy a limited range of activity.

The German Democratic Republic, a state sometimes accused of being "more Marxist than Moscow," has reached a form of accommodation with the Protestant majority. Some degree of church life is permitted, but basic socialist goals cannot be challenged. High-level contacts between government and church authorities have taken place regularly and have eased tensions and contributed to better relations. These contacts, however, are low key and circumspect; the official policy of the government follows the Soviet line.

Hungary and Poland share the reputation of being the most liberal states within the socialist bloc. After the Communist takeover of Hungary there was a period of open conflict with the dominant Roman Catholic church. The church's opposition was symbolized by the defiant stance of Jozsef Cardinal Mindszenty. The early stages of the struggle were marked by outspoken resistance and political trials of clergy, but these gave way to quieter opposition and a lower profile by the church. After the Hungarian revolt of 1956 the restrictions on the churches were removed. The revolt, however, was soon crushed by Soviet tanks, and the government of Janos Kadar reimposed restraints on church activities. Somewhat surprisingly, this same regime gradually began to ease these restrictions, and the Hungarian churches supported the "normalization" of relations with the government as being in their best interest. The state visit of Janos Kadar to Pope Paul VI in 1977 was interpreted by both state authorities and church leaders as a sign that better relations were possible on even the highest levels.

Poland's situation is without parallel in the Eastern bloc. For a thousand years the Roman Catholic church has influenced every aspect of Polish life. As a result, the Communist regime had to take seriously Catholic power from the outset. Although the Polish constitution specifically decrees the separation of church and state, the reality is less clear-cut. It is reported that even many Communists are practicing Catholics. Polish Marxists no longer deny either to themselves or to others that the masses of the people are religious. The role of the church during the unrest associated with the Solidarity movement and its aftermath is powerful testimony to the influence of the Catholic church in contemporary Polish life.

The two countries which have enjoyed the greatest freedom to experiment with new forms of Marxism are Czechoslovakia and Yugoslavia. In the case of the former this freedom was short-lived. For a few brief months in 1968, the reform movement known as the "Prague Spring" created the possibility of Christians working together with Marxists to create "socialism with a human face." The experiment died with the intervention of Eastern bloc troops, and a more traditional Marxist regime was installed. The question which this brief movement posed continues to tantalize the imagination: What if the Dubcek government had succeeded in carrying out its reforms? Would a new and more hopeful form of Christian-Marxist relationship have come into existence? It is unfortunate that the world will never know what might have been.

Initially, following World War II, Yugoslavia followed the same pattern as other East European states. Conflict between church and the government was superceded by a suspension of hostilities and a growing rapprochement. This easing of tensions was complicated by the fact that diverse nationalities, each with its own indigenous church, were united during this period into a single nation. Tito sought to build a sense of national identity by stressing the peculiarities of Yugoslav culture, and in the process created his own version of Marxist-Leninism. This departure from Marxist "orthodoxy" was marked by a peculiarly Yugoslavian emphasis upon decentralization and "self-management." These in turn led to greater freedom of expression for individuals and the churches. The government's official attitude toward the churches has oscillated between periods of greater constraint and periods of increased cooperation. With respect to this relationship, Yugoslavia has perhaps the most interesting potential for development of any of the East European states.

The Emergence of Democratic Socialism

We return to the early years of the 20th century in order to follow the growth of another form of Marxism. World War I proved to be a watershed in the development of European socialism. During the time when the Bolsheviks were consolidating their power in Russia, other socialists saw the democratic process as more than an avenue to political power. They came to accept democracy as good in itself, they argued that socialists should support it, and that socialist goals should be modified in terms of what was compatible with democracy.

This "democratic socialism," as it was called, meant the abandonment of the idea of an ideologically uniform society. Some future "dictatorship of the proletariat" lost its former appeal, and the adherents of this movement worked toward the gradual modification of existing economic systems rather than their overthrow. Continuing to oppose what they saw as the evils of capitalism, these socialists were far less doctrinaire than Marxist-Leninists about private ownership, the market economy, and profit-motivated enterprise. Factors other than those associated with the capitalist means of production were viewed as important for social change.

The split between democratic socialists and communists widened. The former saw communism, because of its use of political coercion and violence, not as a variant form of socialism but its denial. Communists, on the other hand, declared that democratic socialism was a betrayal of the Marxist vision because it recognized the political rights of nonsocialists and had accepted the limitation of traditional socialist goals.

By 1890 the Socialist party in Germany had survived a period of persecution and had become the strongest workers' movement in Europe. As was noted in an earlier chapter, Marx and Engels criticized this party because of the alleged ambiguity of its program. These suspicions may have had some confirmation when, at the outbreak of World War I, the socialists abandoned their rhetoric about the international solidarity of workers and voted with the other parties to support the war effort. After the war, the majority of the party cooperated with nonsocialists in establishing a liberal democratic constitution. This led to repeated charges by Marxist-Leninists that they had betrayed the socialist cause. In reality the German socialists were the most trustworthy supporters of German democracy until the advent of nazism in 1933.

The Nazi takeover of Germany was hastened by the split between the communists and the socialists, whose energies were devoted more to conflict with one another than opposition to fascism. Shortly after Hitler came to power, all socialist and communist organizations were outlawed. The leaders of these parties who did not leave the country were thrown into prison and concentration camps or murdered. Yet on the eve of the Nazi victory in March 1933, the Communist party publicly declared, "Each vote for the German Socialist party is a vote for Hitler!" The consequences of this intra-Marxist struggle were disastrous for both parties.

Western European Socialism in the Postwar Era

Following the defeat of the Nazis, the democratic socialists and the labor unions participated in the political and economic reconstruction of West Germany, or the German Federal Republic, as it came to be called. Developments in East Germany (the German Democratic Republic) fueled strong anticommunist sentiment, and in 1956 the Federal Constitutional Court prohibited the small communist party. With a membership of less than 40,000 persons and little electoral success, the party never had the influence of the communist parties in France and Italy. In 1960 the German socialists declared themselves to be a *Volkspartei,* or people's party, and came to be known as the Social Democratic party. Under the leadership of Willy Brandt and Helmut Schmidt they enjoyed considerable electoral success and were the ruling party in West Germany for a number of years.[6]

A somewhat different process occurred on the other side of the Rhine. French democratic socialists won power briefly as senior partners in the Popular Front of 1936, a coalition which also included liberals and communists. The socialists, however, failed to reformulate their ideology and programs to reflect the priority of democracy over socialism and so remained largely Marxist until after World War II. This has changed significantly in the postwar period. Under the leadership of Francois Mitterand, French socialists, in cooperation with the communists, have broken the hold of the various center-right parties on the government and now govern France. Socialist policies have met with a mixed reaction from the French electorate, but Mitterand has demonstrated a strong orientation to the Western democracies in international affairs.

The French Communist party (PCF) has grown to become the second largest communist party in Western Europe. Its phenomenal success has stemmed in part from the "policy of the open hand" inaugurated by party leader Maurice Thorez in 1937 during the government of the Popular Front. He was succeeded in more recent times by Georges Marchais who, like Thorez, held the influential post of secretary-general of the PCF.

In a 1976 address captioned "Appeal to the Christians of France," Marchais spoke of a change in the "system in which grand capital exercises its dominion over every aspect of national life.''[7] Nevertheless, Marchais assured his audience of more than 10,000 persons, the political change which the PCF proposed was ''modern democracy.'' This ''modern democracy'' was to be both economic and political. On the economic level, power would pass from the hands of the privileged minority of grand capitalists ''into the hands of the nation, to be put solely at the service of our people.''[8] On the political level, power would be held by those who were productive and who would serve the common good. The road to this modern democracy would be based on ''the democratic expression of the popular will,'' and would be respected by the communists whatever the electoral outcome.

Skeptics have wondered whether the policy of the PCF represented a genuine modification of Marxist ideology or whether it was a propaganda ploy designed to attract the masses of noncommunist workers to the Marxist camp. This suspicion was heightened by PCF support of the Soviet invasion of Afghanistan and the suppression of the Solidarity movement in Poland. Nevertheless, the fact remains that for more than 40 years the policy of the open hand has been the official stance of the party, and that this policy has opened the door to continued dialogue among communists, Catholics, and democratic socialists.

A somewhat different situation exists in the most communist nation in Western Europe. Italy may be the first and perhaps the only NATO state to achieve a parliamentary majority of communists. This possibility, together with the powerful and traditional role of the Roman Catholic church in that nation, makes the position of the Communist party of Italy (PCI) unique among communist parties.

In 1976, Enrico Berlinguer, secretary-general of the PCI, addressed a meeting of communist parties convened in East Berlin with the forthright declaration that ''We struggle for a socialist society that is built upon the assertion of personal as well as collective freedom.''[9] According to Berlinguer, such a state would permit a plurality of parties in order to provide leadership alternatives, allow religious freedom, and not hinder the contributions of private initiative to the development of the economy. This from the leader of the Communist party! Berlinguer then took the remarkable step of pledging support for a coalition government led by the Christian Democrats; his initiative was promptly labeled the ''historic compromise.''[10] By 1980 the Italian Communist leader had opened a campaign to establish ties with the socialist and other moderate European parties. His efforts met with the strong disapproval of the Soviets and the more traditional Marxist-Leninists.

The Marxist Adaptation to Parliamentary Democracy

The attempts of the PCI to liberalize the Italian brand of Marxism put severe strains on what came to be called "Eurocommunism," a loose alliance of Western European Marxists who sought alternatives to Soviet-style Marxist-Leninism. Following the lead of the Italian and Spanish communist parties, the Eurocommunists called for policies that would be "equidistant from the policies of the United States and the Soviet Union."[11] This effort at compromise, however, began to falter when the French communists discovered that the Socialist party was gaining strength at their expense. The Spanish communists also failed to benefit from this movement, and have lost support at a steady rate since their party was legalized after the death of Francisco Franco. In recent times its numbers have dropped to fewer than 140,000 members. Even the larger PCI has suffered at the polls in recent years. Whether Eurocommunism has a future remains to be seen.

While Western European communists were struggling to adapt to parliamentary systems, the democratic socialists of Great Britain, Scandinavia, and the Low Countries more easily adjusted Marxist ideology to the requirements of democracy. Universal suffrage and the rules of representative democracy put democratic socialists in power first in Sweden, then in Norway and Denmark and, in coalition with other parties, in Finland. Scandinavian democratic socialists nationalized very few private enterprises. The public sector of the economy was expected to compete with the private, cooperativism was encouraged, the allocation of resources was regulated, public services were expanded, and labor and social legislation improved. Today the Scandinavian countries, among the most socialized states in Western Europe, enjoy some of the highest standards of living in the world.

Because of its proximity to the Soviet Union, Finland represents a unique case. Finland became an independent nation in 1917, but independence was followed by a bitter civil war. The labor movement was well organized prior to World War I and had shown its strength in the "Great Strike" of 1905. The civil war led to the defeat of the socialist forces, and the Lutheran church of Finland ranged itself almost totally on the side of the "Whites" versus the "Reds." This fact is still remembered by contemporary Finnish socialists.[12]

During World War II Finland was forced into a war with the Soviet Union. The Soviet victory led to the annexation of some Finnish territory and the imposition of a harsh treaty in 1944. Postwar foreign policy was geared to political neutrality. Opposition to communism continues to be deeply rooted in large sectors of the general population. The Communist party, however, is a well-established part of national political life, and is divided into the "revisionist" and "neo-Stalinist" factions. For a short period during the 1960s, Finland even had a "Popular Front" government which included socialists, communists, and representatives of some other parties. Communists in this country apparently have adjusted to their role in a democratic society and hold a significant number of parliamentary seats.

The British Labor party came to power in 1924 and again, with a somewhat greater plurality, in 1929. To a large extent the party adopted the socialist position of the Fabian Society, which stood firmly for democratic procedure, and advocated a mixed economy instead of collectivism, the nationalization of certain basic industries, comprehensive social and labor legislation, redistribution of income through governmental action, and the breakup of large fortunes by means of taxation. Following its electoral successes in 1945, the Labor party adopted the economic policies of Beveridge and Keyes, and instituted far-reaching social changes, particularly in education. The result was the establishment of an extensive welfare society in which the government had a larger role than in the American New Deal but a lesser one than governments in the collectivist economics of Eastern Europe. British socialists have always looked to a strong trade union movement for essential political support. In recent years their internal disputes have led to the emergence of a centrist Social Democratic party, composed of dissident Labor party members and the small Liberal party. The continuing division of liberal-left political forces in Great Britain has done much to assure the retention of power by the ruling Conservative party.

Varieties of Marxism in the United States

While Marxism has never enjoyed numerical success in the United States, it nevertheless has influenced a long and rich tradition of social-democratic labor movements. Even before its appearance, a Workers' party came on the scene briefly in 1828. The National Reform party was organized in 1872, the Social Democratic party in 1873, only to be replaced in 1877 by the Socialist Labor party.[13] Agreement in 1900 between the new Social Democratic party led by Eugene V. Debs and splinter groups from the Socialist Labor party led to the formation of the American Socialist party. While it enjoyed limited electoral success just before and after World War I, this movement did not become a significant political factor on the American scene. The Socialist party presidential candidate in 1920, Eugene V. Debs, received just under a million votes. While his successor, the former Presbyterian minister Norman Thomas, attracted almost 900,000 votes in the depression year election of 1932, the Socialist party never again exhibited comparable strength. The social programs of the New Deal undercut what support it sought to gain from American workers. Nevertheless, the proposals of the Socialist party, especially under the leadership of Norman Thomas, influenced the political platforms of both major parties. Today its aims are furthered through the activities of the Democratic Socialists of America. Led by the social activist and scholar, Michael Harrington, that organization works closely with progressive elements in the Democratic party.

The American Communist party identified closely with the Bolshevik movement after it came to power in Russia. For a time it attracted intellectuals who believed that a new and promising society was being shaped by the Communist party in the Soviet Union. Its electoral strength never approached that of the Socialist party, although in the 1932 election the communist candidate, William Z. Foster, received more than 102,000 votes. Communist attempts to forge a "common front" with other parties against European fascism were successful at first but were undermined by the Soviet and Nazi nonaggression pact at the end of the 1930s. The subservience of American communists to Moscow and revelations of Stalinist terror contributed to the party's steady decline. Presiding over the changing fortunes of the American Communist party during the years before and after the Second World War were William Z. Foster, Earl Browder, and Gus Hall. Further weakened by defections during the McCarthy era, the party today is known chiefly through its publication *The Daily Worker*.

A number of Marxist splinter movements have emerged in recent years. Perhaps the most important is the Socialist Workers party, a group known for its adherence to Trotsky's views. Other elements have been influenced by the thought of Mao or other Third World Marxists. Anarchist tendencies have not been entirely absent in some of these groups.

In the 1960s a new political phenomenon made its appearance in North America and parts of Western Europe. Reviving some of the 19th-century arguments against bourgeois democracy, this movement was also distrustful of orthodox Marxist-Leninism. Its socialist roots and tendencies were evident in its critique of modern industrial society. Known as the "New Left," its "revisionist" character provoked the distrust of more traditional Marxists. Ideologically, this movement was close to the views of 19th-century socialists like Blanqui and Proudhon. Most of its support came from young persons who were unaware of earlier debates between socialists and nonsocialists or among the socialists themselves. Reflecting a variety of influences from the emerging counterculture, the New Left had largely exhausted its potential by the end of the 1970s. It made few lasting contributions to socialist thought and practice in the Western industrial nations.

6 Marxism and Christianity in Asia

by Paul V. Martinson

Marxism does not seem to be a serious contender in the economic, political, or intellectual scene in North America. However, this is not the case in much of the rest of the world. Nearly one-half of the world's people live within countries whose governments claim to be Marxist. The vast majority of these countries have become Marxist states since World War II, and, indeed, the vast majority of these people live in the Third World. Marxism for many is a serious option.

Can so many people be wrong? We may hardly think this question is worth asking; yet, can we fail to ask it if we are to be honest with ourselves and with the world?

Scholars often like to draw the distinction between Marxism (as a system of thought) and communism (as a political system), and argue that it is improper to judge the one from the other. *Communism* commonly refers to states that are founded upon a Marxist-Leninist ideology and practice: Russia, China, Cuba, and Mozambique come to mind. The Leninist version—or perversion as it more often may be suggested—of Marxism is only one form of communism, and its excesses and distortions ought not preclude our consideration of Marxism as a serious intellectual and practical proposal for our world today. In contrast to the state ideology of communism, Marxism is not to be viewed as a set of eternal truths chiseled in stone, but as a dynamic set of insights that give us a perspective on the world. These insights, moreover, do not necessarily prejudge the precise way we might achieve that better world of justice and hope for all.

This view of Marxism is correct, but it is also a bit abstract. Marxism is evident in active political and economic systems which trace their intellectual heritage to Marx and govern so many of the world's people. Whether or not these systems conform with some scholar's "idealist" version of Marxism is hardly relevant; that they inform the lives of many with a "real" version is a compelling fact.

There are two ways to proceed in this discussion. One way is to begin with a dynamic set of ideas that have not been truly realized anywhere anytime, but perhaps ought to be; another way is to begin with an actual set of social, political, and economic practices that claim to be realizations truly inspired by the thought of Marx. Some social democratic proposals, and certainly the liberation theology proposals of Latin America, represent the former; the communist states that are securely in place China and Cuba, for instance—represent the latter. The procedure of this essay will be to begin with the "facts" and conclude with the hopes.

As a nation we are still trying to come to terms with the fact that immediately after World War II one-fourth of the world's people became communist overnight. These events are spoken of as "liberation." This is not without reason; a long history of oppression and injustice preceeded the liberation. Marxist-inspired ideas of liberation had already yeasted in Asia for some decades. Although we might find it difficult to understand, the Russian revolution of 1917 was an electrifying event in much of Asia. Prior to this Marx was virtually unknown there; but after this revolution his thoughts quickly became widespread.

This revolution spawned communist parties throughout the world, including Asia. The Indonesian Communist party, the earliest in Asia, anticipated that revolution, having been organized in 1914 (in 1920 it took the name "Communist") under the inspiration of the Dutch Marxist Sneevliet. About the time of the Russian revolution, M. N. Roy, an exiled Indian Marxist, organized a party while in Mexico, though the formal establishment of the Communist party of India took place in 1928; an embryo Korean Communist party was organized in 1918 among Korean exiles in Siberia; in 1919 (the same year as it occurred in the United States) a party was organized amongst peasants and laborers in the Philippines; in China in 1921 a small group of intellectuals, amongst them Mao Zedong, gathered in Shanghai to found the Chinese Communist party. In a few years time, parties had been organized in most

Asian countries. Ho Chi Minh amalgamated several groups in 1930 to form the Communist party of Indochina (Vietnam). Meanwhile, the Communist International (the Comintern) founded by Lenin in 1919 (dissolved in 1943) to promote world revolution encouraged Marxist ferment in Asia in service of the interests of the Russian revolution.

None of this happened in a vacuum, and this is where the story really begins. What made the Russian revolution such a welcome event to many in Asia was not that it was a Marxist revolution but that the situation of oppression in Russia within which it occurred reminded them of their own situation, and lent them hope for their own liberation. The Russian revolution was a sign of promise.

What was the situation in Asia? Colonialism was certainly the dominant political fact: England ruling India, Burma, Ceylon, and Malaya; France ruling Indochina; Holland ruling Indonesia; the United States ruling in the Philippines; not to mention a host of lesser colonial holdings by these and other western nations. Even Czarist Russia had begun in the late 19th century to push eastwards across central Asia, confronting both China and Japan on their northern borders. The superficial peace imposed from without often hid or prolonged already existing tensions and introduced a whole host of new ones. Long-standing ethnic, cultural, and religious animosities lay hidden from view, if still smouldering. Amongst these were Hindu-Muslim tensions throughout the Indian subcontinent; resentment throughout Southeast Asia toward enterprising Chinese minorities; long-standing ethnic rivalries throughout Indochina; Muslim-Catholic tensions in the Philippines. Moreover, the general poverty of 19th- and 20th-century Asia with its crushing population growth was made all the more evident by a new class of wealth and power introduced by the colonizing West. For good or for ill, colonialism introduced a heady mixture of new and powerful ingredients—new ideas, new technologies, new possibilities, most notably that of industrialization. Education, much of it through schools established by Christian missions, played a particularly significant role in introducing these new ideas. Among other things, this potent mixture resulted in a growing resentment of western dominance that fueled nascent nationalist aspirations, not infrequently rupturing the colonial facade with rebellion and revolution.

The Russian revolution with its antiimperialist and anticapitalist rhetoric backed by successful revolutionary action, caught the imagination of many intellectuals in Asia. Well before the success of the revolution Lenin had already persuasively argued the case. Commenting on the

Boxer Uprising in China in 1900 Lenin accused the European capitalists and their governments of plunder. He wrote:

> This policy of plunder has become known as colonial policy. Every country in which capitalist industry is developing has to seek colonies, i.e. countries in which industry is weakly developed, in which more or less patriarchal conditions still prevail, which can serve as a market for manufactured goods and a source of high profits. In the interests of a handful of capitalists, the bourgeois governments have waged endless wars, have kept regiments of soldiers in torment in unhealthy tropical countries, have squandered millions of money extracted from the people, and have brought the people in the colonies to a state of desperate revolt or to death from starvation.

For those who were on the receiving end of colonialism the case could hardly have been more convincingly argued.

To be sure, other factors were at work besides the inspiration of revolutionary Russia, and though Marxist ideas became widespread in Asia not all peoples threw off colonialism to become communist. India, the Philippines, Burma, and Indonesia are representative. But others did throw off the mantle of colonialism to become Marxist-Leninist states.

Japan played a unique role in this mixture. As early as the Meiji Restoration of 1868 it chose western-style modernization. Japan's brush with western colonialism was not all that serious —for a few brief years it had to grant extraterritorial rights to western nations. Meanwhile it had learned the western trick and became a colonial power in its own right. Korea and China first felt Japan's ambitions—in 1895 China was defeated in a war with Japan—and by 1905 even Russia had been defeated militarily. Japan, however, was never really fully accepted into the colonial "club," but always felt like the odd one out. Various treaties kept its military strength to a lesser level, and the galling United States Immigration Law of 1924 blatantly discriminated against Asians—including the Japanese. Meanwhile, a new Japanese nationalism evolved that was devoted ideologically to the emperor, and with this gradually developed the idea that Japan could become the great deliverer of Asia.

As World War II demonstrated, Japan failed to take into account at least two crucial factors: the national and religious self-consciousness that was sweeping Asia from India to the Philippines, and the untested resolve and military might of the United States. With the defeat of Japan and the failure of its attempt to deliver Asia, the colonial map of Asia shattered into its many pieces, the puzzle was never to be put together again: India, under the influence of Ghandi and other national leaders, resisted English rule, Indochina resisted French rule, Indonesia resisted Dutch rule, and so the matter went. The fallout was an Asia largely free from colonial rule and the advent of major Communist nations—China, Vietnam, and North Korea.

Our involvement in each of these cases—despair at the Chinese nationalist defeat, stalemate in Korea, humiliation in Vietnam—has not kindly disposed us towards Asian communism. But time shows it to be a changing reality, and the assumptions of the past do not necessarily hold good for the future. The Nixon-Kissinger/Mao-Chou inspired detente of the 1972 "Shanghai Communique" marked an epoch in our relations with communism in Asia—the warfare of the past slowly yields to economic cooperation as we enter the future of an increasingly important Pacific Economic Basin.

Four general comments may sum up our learning from the past and our entry into the future. First, nationalism has profoundly shaped Asian communism such that national identity limits, if it does not prevail over, communist unity. The myth of a monolithic worldwide communist conspiracy, whatever the rhetoric, has been shattered. Like a huge reptile swallowing its own tail, China threatened Vietnam, which subdued the Communists of Cambodia, who devoured their own people, the same devourers who were supported by China. Looming over this circle of conflict is the Russo-Chinese rivalry and the uncertainties of Korea on one wing of Asia and Afghanistan on the other.

Second, these national communisms are deeply committed to their own brand of Marxist-Leninist socialism. This commitment, while real, has by no means been an untroubled one. China affords a classic example.

It will be worthwhile to briefly elaborate this example. We live in the post-Mao era, just as we live in the post-Stalin era. Mao Zedong became the unchallenged hero of the Chinese revolution but, as it turned out, represented an ever leftward moving idealism. Socialism in its broadest sense refers to all social movements and ideas that seek to maximize cooperative and communitarian ways of humans living together. This necessarily has to do with economic life, for here cooperative and noncooperative ways of living together find their final practical test. Mao, who won his spurs as a creative communist leader by welding peasant revolt into the service of a proletarian revolution, sought, upon the success of the revolution, to leap over the capitalist and socialist phases of history as outlined in "orthodox" Marxist thought and attain the realm of spontaneous and universal cooperation of pure communism in one fell swoop. The now infamous Cultural Revolution (1966-1976) marked the dizzying climax and unraveling of this utopian vision. Up to this time the Chinese revolution, which established a government in Peking in 1949, had started its program in the largely agrarian society of China in a dramatic, yet economically "conservative" way, by dispossessing all landlords and distributing their land to individual farming families. This initial move towards private property (part of the design) was soon reversed in the movement to develop cooperatives whereby farmers voluntarily, even if by persuasion, gave up certain rights to land and implement use so as to share these usages with others. This led in the late 1950s to communization, a system in which all land, implements, and products were the sole possession of the state. When this outward transformation of society did not eliminate self-interest and lead to the ideal of a spontaneous and universal altruism, Mao unleashed the Cultural Revolution to seize the political initiative and to bring about an inward transformation of the people.

As we all know, this action by Mao led to a disastrous failure. As a result, the once infallible "thought of Mao" has been reevaluated and placed in historical perspective. Mao, being human, could err. However, this reevaluation did not lead to a rejection of socialism as method and goal. The "four maintains" espoused by the party and enshrined in the latest constitution (1982) are taken very seriously in China—the socialist path, the guiding role of Marxism-Leninism and Mao Zedong thought, the dictatorship of the proletariat, and (most important of all) the leadership of the Chinese Communist party. These four items set the outer limits within which the current reforms (the so-called four modernizations, namely, those in industry, agriculture, science/technology, and defense) are to be pursued. Nevertheless, this permits significant changes from past practice. In agriculture this means that implementation of state ownership of land has been effectively modified. Today the emphasis is upon individual and small group (not just state) management of public land. In many cases the only difference between state and private ownership is that land cannot be held title to or alienated—privately bought or sold. Similar tendencies are at work transforming the conduct of industry in China and making possible joint ventures with overseas capitalists.

The failures of Chinese communism have been accompanied by noteworthy successes as well. Although abundance awaits as a possibility still to be worked toward, and our conception of human individual rights has not become a reality, distributive justice has been quite effectively achieved as well as equal access to basic human services. India and China, the two most populous nations on earth, can make a thought provoking comparison here. A renewed pride in being Chinese has developed. Despite the troubles of the recent past, few in China would wish to return to the prerevolutionary days. One could almost say that today to be Chinese is to be socialist.

The third comment concerns the church. The fortunes of the church in North Korea and Vietnam are not as well known as those of the church in China in recent (past four) years. Although the church in China composed a super-minority (less than 1%), and experienced severe repression for a time, it has in fact grown. With the commitment of the Marxist state to granting a measured but genuine religious freedom, the church has become stronger than ever and continues to grow at an astonishing rate. A socialist state (even of the Marxist-Leninist variety) and a vigorous church are not necessarily mutually exclusive.

Finally, while we have primarily referred to state socialisms, these do not represent the only influence of Marxism in Asia, or in the Third World, for that matter. In India, Marxist commitments have had a dominant influence at state and local politics in several places; the governmental policies of Sri Lanka (Ceylon) have been largely shaped by Marxist ideas; socialism in Burma, while grounded in Buddhist commitments, has also been partially shaped by Marxist inspirations. Furthermore, the active role of Communist parties in national politics and the ferment stirred by Marxist ideas continues throughout Asia. Continued economic inequities and the political oppression of such aggressively anti-Communist governments as those of South Korea, the Philippines, and Taiwan continue to fuel these stirrings.

We have considered briefly the existence of "real" versions of Marxism in Asia. But these realities are not unrelated to some fundamental ideals and hopes that give them plausibility. Elsewhere in this book the fundamental inspirations that Marx articulated and their relevance—perhaps increasing relevance—for us today are dealt with. History and theology (thinking in a Christian way about the meaning of events) are not to be divorced.

We can conclude this brief historical reflection by referring once again to the case of China. For most in the church both inside and outside of China the triumph of communism there was considered to be an unparalleled disaster. There were those who dissented, such as Wu Yaozong, the later founder of the Three-Self movement in China, the predecessor body of the present church. He spoke of this as a cleansing event in which "God has taken the key of salvation from the church and given it to another." For him, practical religion became almost identified with socialist action and the rediscovery of "Chinesehood."

Wu Yaozong died in 1979, and a new generation of leaders now succeeds him. Less radical in their sentiments—after all there was a Cultural Revolution!—basic national and socialist convictions have not been discarded. Bishop Ding, the present chairperson of the Chinese Christian Council, reflects in a recent book published in China (1982) upon his early encounter with Mr. Wu in the days before the revolution: "There I stood," he writes, "with a Greek word list stuffed in one pocket, and with some studies on the '39 Articles' of the Church of England, now some centuries old, stuffed in the other. The education I received at that time led me to become immersed in problems of the divine and human natures of Christ, his place and function in redemption, and so on. The way Mr. Wu with his Christology brought Jesus back into present history and present reality was entirely new to me and opened up for me in my Christian faith a realm hitherto unknown." Referring to "liberation theology" Ding observes that Wu was "without question a precursor" of this later development in spirit if not in fact.

Now, however, in the words of Ding, China is in a "postrevolutionary" situation. The central issue is no longer simply liberation but "reconciliation," above all with the Chinese people, and at the same time with the socialist revolution. Reflecting on his intimate discussions with Wu in the 50s and 60s over breakfasts of fish and gruel, Ding continues: Mr. Wu had a profound respect for Paul who "peeled the Jewish husk from off the gospel of Christ," and thereby made it available to the whole world. The doctrine of "justification by faith" was a formula of reconciliation, not alienation. But in China the gospel has appeared foreign and alienating by virtue of its past identification with colonialism. It used to be said, "One more Christian, one less Chinese." Communism in China has restored a sense of Chinese identity, with Christians included in this Chinese self-discovery. Ding makes the remarkable comparison that as Paul created the theological conditions for a Jewish and Gentile reconciliation—which offered a hope never to be fulfilled—Wu in his development of a truly national Chinese church has for the Chinese people performed "a comparable creative act opening up a new state in history," such that the Christian faith "might become, without any sense of shame, the religious faith of the people of our independent, socialist ancestral land."

The past century in Asia has been an age of epochal change, passing through the phases of colonialism, nationalism, independence, and in some cases communism, and now to a day that calls for a new sense of interdependence and reconciliation. The ancient Confucian epigram still applies: "Our burden is great and our journey long; humanity is our burden, is it not a heavy one? Death marks the end of our journey, is it not a long one?"

Christian Encounter
with Marxism

7 The Christian-Marxist Encounter in the West

by Paul T. Jersild

Having considered the ideas of Karl Marx and the historical development of those ideas in various countries, we turn now to the Christian response to Marxism. In this chapter we will note first the various reactions to Marxism found in North American Christianity, and then focus on the dialogues between Christians and Marxists in various Western countries. Rather than describing each of these dialogues, our primary concern is to raise the question of their importance and validity as well as to note the common themes which emerge from them.

The Response to Marxism in American Christianity

Most Christians in America are not particularly informed about the thinking of Karl Marx. The ideas of Marx are identified with communism, and lack of knowledge on the part of most people does not permit them to discriminate between the two. Communism in turn makes us think of Russia and the threat which that nation poses for the United States in a nuclear showdown. It is communism as we perceive it in this context of political and military confrontation which shapes our reaction to Marxism.

The Christian Far Right

It is understandable therefore that many, if not most, Christians respond to Marxism with apprehension, and that numerous groups bearing the name of Christian have advocated a belligerent approach to communism. Two well-known organizations dating back to the post-World War II years which represent this stance are the Christian crusade of

Billy James Hargis and the Christian anticommunist crusade of Fred Schwarz. Both men regard themselves as called to reveal to a naive American public how totally demonic communism is. They skillfully play on the fears of people, creating an atmosphere which would regard any attempt at dialogue with Marxists as either evil or stupid.

Such a view displays a gross sense of self-righteousness incapable of recognizing that evil can be found on both sides of any conflict. It assumes that either side must be absolutely right or absolutely wrong. Billy James Hargis makes clear who is wrong with his assertion that Marx's teachings are actually a manifestation of Satan:

> It is apparent upon examination that Communism cannot be of human origin, for human beings are of themselves incapable of total corruption. Only Satan could inspire in human beings complete dedication to utter folly, unspeakable horrors, and total untruth. Only Satan can be the inspiration of Communism.[1]

One can discount this kind of talk as typical of a lunatic fringe, and yet even the president of the United States has said that Soviet communism is "the focus of evil in the modern world." This kind of sentiment has had a deep impact on the American consciousness, helping to create a profound suspicion of anything remotely associated with Marxism. It has encouraged us to think in terms of sweeping stereotypes which have prevented us from understanding the dynamic behind this movement. It has encouraged a closed mind on issues associated with the Marxist critique of Western society—issues of poverty and wealth, economic justice, aspirations of freedom, and the legitimacy of revolution on the part of oppressed people in many parts of the world.

These observations are not intended to deny or minimize the serious flaws to be found in Marxism. Indeed, self-righteousness and the inability to maintain self-criticism are often obvious among Marxists, particularly where a communist regime has come into power. The oppressive totalitarianism that has developed in numerous communist countries is more than ample evidence of this fact. But are Christians justified in stripping Marxists of their humanity by identifying them with Satanic powers? The clear implication is that so-called Christian nations are justified in taking whatever measures they think necessary to destroy this enemy, creating the frightful prospect of a "holy war" in the nuclear age.

The anticommunist crusades in this country tended to run out of steam in the 1970s as we became aware that worldwide communism was not a monolithic power but was wracked by severe internal divisions. The serious rift between Russia and China has dramatized this fact. While various anticommunist groups continue on, many of the people to whom they appeal have become preoccupied with other issues. They are active in such groups as the Moral Majority, which emerged as a political factor in the 1980 elections. While the concerns of these people have broadened considerably, their stance on communism remains adamant and is reflected in their solid support for an increased military budget. Jerry Falwell's message may not be as bellicose and extreme as that of Hargis, but he represents the same concerns and has actually succeeded in gathering far more public support for a rigorous anticommunist stance.

Another phenomenon which has contributed to the mentality we are discussing is the popularity of various writers who have attempted to relate the apocalyptic literature in the Bible (Daniel, Revelation) to our own times. Capitalizing on the fears of people living in the nuclear age, writers like Hal Lindsey *(The Late Great Planet Earth)* claim to reveal the secrets of the future with its impending struggle between the forces of good and evil. This cosmic confrontation—the biblical Armageddon—is pictured as a showdown between the Communist East and the Christian West, once again encouraging the idea that the followers of Marx are the ultimate enemies of the children of God.

Mainline Denominations

The response of mainline denominations to worldwide communism generally has not been as strident. Most churches addressed the threat of communism in the early 1960s through statements issued by their departments of church and society. These documents give ample attention to the menace communism poses to American ideals of democracy and freedom, but there is also recognition of our responsibility as citizens and particularly as Christians. The point is made that opposition to communism is not enough; positive action is needed. The ideals of our own political tradition must be lived out in our lives and in the policies of our nation.

The distinction is also made between communism as an ideology and the people who live under Communist governments. As one statement puts it, "It is important for Christians to remember that while we condemn and reject the system of communism, we still share in God's love for the people living under the regime." Recognition is also made of the fact that Christians are obligated to study and inform themselves about Marxist communism. While these statements are generally quite sweeping in their denunciation of communism, there is also the expression of a desire to distinguish between truth and falsehood in our understanding of it.

As we noted, the anticommunist hysteria of the 50s and 60s subsided to some extent in the 70s, and this is reflected in the relative absence of church statements on communism during that decade. The most recent statement from the National Conference of Catholic Bishops (their ''Pastoral Letter on Marxist Communism,'' dated November 12, 1980) reveals a significantly different stance and tone from earlier denominational statements. Professing to be not a polemical or political tract but a Christian reflection on the Marxist world view, this statement devotes far more attention to understanding the actual thought of Marx. It concludes that the Achilles heel of Marxism is its absence of moral absolutes which provide a safeguard against the often oppressive goals of the party or an individual leader. The norm cannot simply be identified with the views of those in power.

In the closing pages of the ''Pastoral Letter,'' the question is raised, ''Must the opposition between Marxist theory and Christian doctrine always remain antagonistic?'' It answers this question by saying that it is impossible to give a definitive answer. But because Marxism has a very practical orientation which leads to changes in its adaptation to the environment, it is at least an open question and the possibility of understanding and mutual cooperation should not be ruled out. Changes in practice can force changes in theory. For a Roman Catholic statement to express this kind of openness is certainly significant; it gives hope that the Christian response to Marxism in this country will increasingly demonstrate more understanding and point us beyond wary coexistence.

Influential Theologians

In addition to the Far Right and mainline denominations, it is worthwhile to note briefly the response to Marxism of several influential theologians because of the impact they have had on the thinking of both clergy and laity. We will note here the response of just two of North America's most prominent theologians, both of them firmly rooted in the Reformation tradition: Reinhold Niebuhr and Paul Tillich.

While serving a working class parish in Detroit from 1915 to 1928, Niebuhr became a socialist. In the 1930s he became disenchanted with the ideological struggles going on within the Socialist party and finally left it. While never joining the Communist party, he regarded as valid the Marxist critique of capitalism and thought that Marxism would provide ''the only possible property system compatible with the necessities of a technical age."[2] But Niebuhr was sensitive to the totalitarian character of communism in Stalinist Russia, concluding that Marxism itself was at fault in its understanding of political power. No ideology that allowed such a ruthless misuse of power could be sanctioned by the Christian.

Though sympathetic to certain elements in Marxist thought, Niebuhr's development of his own position—called "Christian realism"—resulted in a critical judgment of the utopianism in Marx. Niebuhr was sensitive to the pervasiveness of pride in human relationships, making even the most noble visions of social justice subject to the selfish limitations of those in power. This made him critical of optimistic views of human nature and grand schemes for the solving of human problems, whether they were proposed by Marxists or liberals of the Western democratic tradition. He assumed a pragmatic view of the political process, rejecting idealistic visions of a new order and coming to appreciate the modest, yet concrete measures of Roosevelt's New Deal in behalf of the working class.[3]

Paul Tillich, a native of Germany, was suspended from his teaching position at the University of Frankfurt in 1933 as a result of his outspoken criticism of nazism. At the invitation of Niebuhr he came later that year to Union Theological Seminary in New York, avoiding likely imprisonment in his homeland. Tillich was always an astute observer of and participant in the political and social scene. While in Germany he became a socialist and recognized with appreciation the idealism and zeal for reform that were present in the early Marx. He thought it important that the church understand the basis of Marxist thought, maintaining that one could interpret communism itself as a secularized and politicized form of certain prophetic values that one can find in the Christian tradition.

Tillich was impressed with the analogies between Marxism and Christianity. Particularly in regard to the understanding of human nature and of history, Marx was clearly influenced by Christian thought. His view of human life as alienated and estranged reflects in part the Christian understanding of the Fall, and his view of history as linear with a unique goal and fulfillment reflects the Christian conviction that history is moving towards an *eschaton* prepared by the God of history. At the same time, Tillich stressed the contrasts between Marxism and Christianity. He saw a fatal flaw in the fact that Marx identified an elite with the possession of the truth, resulting in the totalitarian excesses of a Stalinist Russia. The Marxist view of history betrays the same naivete in its uncritical designation of the proletariat as the messianic bearer of a new order. In both instances the loss of a transcendent God results in the "divinizing" of a particular group, with all the fateful excesses that result from such a conviction.[4]

As students of Marxism, both Niebuhr and Tillich reveal an honest grappling with the ideas of Marx and a willingness to appreciate their historical roots. Both men are sensitive to the impetus in behalf of social justice inherent to the Christian message, and the consequent need to listen to every voice that cries out for justice and reform. But their assessment of Marx is marked by discrimination; they are willing to be appreciative, but they bring a penetrating critique of what they recognize as crucial flaws in his thought and in the subsequent development of Marxism. The stance of both of them would certainly encourage a critical spirit as well as openness to dialogue on the part of Christians in their relation to Marxists.

The Christian-Marxist Dialogue

Many Christians in the United States would regard dialogue between Christians and Marxists as utterly impossible. There would appear to be no common ground on which the two sides could meet. Many would assume that the only possible purpose of these kinds of meetings would be to convert the Marxists to Christianity. However, such a viewpoint fails to recognize that the very purpose of dialogue is to help both sides break out of that mentality which slices the world into opposing camps, refusing to allow for possibilities of understanding and the recognition of mutual goals.

To engage in genuine dialogue is to be willing to acknowledge that our own side has something to learn. It demands openness to the possibility that Christians as well as Marxists can be guilty of self-interest which prejudices our view of the other side and prevents us from really understanding their aspirations. It is to recognize that they are human beings too, moved by their own vision of the future and what they hope to do for their society and the larger world. It is not surprising that Christian-Marxist dialogues have often been initiated by reform-minded people who have not been a part of official church or party leadership, but who have been moved by what they perceived to be the best interests of both Christians and Marxists, and the world at large.

Historical Development of the Dialogue
Several factors helped create an environment in the 1960s which encouraged the dialogue. The movement toward de-Stalinization among

communists encouraged the recognition that the totalitarianism associated with Stalin was an aberration and that a more open society was desirable. Though not dramatic, a certain relaxing of East-West tensions occurred during this decade in various areas of the West. The Communist parties in Europe began to assume more independence in their relation to Russia. For the churches, the papacy of John XXIII and Vatican Council II were highly significant in creating a more open atmosphere.

The year 1964 saw the dialogue begin, though informally there had been meetings of Christians and Marxists (usually in the context of the university) going back to the late 1950s. Czechoslovakia, Italy, West Germany, and France were countries in which dialogues took place, with an increasing number of participants from each side. Theologians and representatives of various disciplines in the social sciences were present among the Christians, meeting with Marxist philosophers and theoreticians. In Italy a book appeared in 1964 in which the contributors were five Marxists and five Roman Catholics. In West Germany, Austria, and Czechoslovakia, annual meetings were held for five years in a row, in which the participants addressed such themes as "The Christian and Marxist Future," "Christian Humanity and Marxist Humanism," and "Creativity and Freedom in a Humane Society."

The 1968 Russian invasion of Czechoslovakia brought the dialogue to a halt, and in the early 1970s it appeared to many that dialogue was dead. It was then, however, that Latin America began to assume increasing importance with the emergence of liberation theology and cooperative efforts between Christians and Marxists in working for social justice. The interest in Latin America was focused more on concrete activity in behalf of oppressed people rather than on dialogue. But efforts at dialogue have continued in various countries. The Institute of Peace Studies at the University of Vienna and the International Institute for Peace in Vienna have jointly held a number of conferences throughout the '70s attended by Christians and Marxists. At the 1976 East Berlin Conference of European Communist Parties, dialogue and cooperation with Christians were noted approvingly in the final document.

Interest in dialogue in the United States has been minimal for several reasons. Unlike some of the European countries, Marxist presence in this country is hardly visible. What Marxist presence there is, is badly splintered. Thus American Christians have tended to look to Europe for Marxist partners in dialogue. Most recently, the efforts of Prof. Paul Mojzes of Rosemont College and the organization CAREE (Christians Associated for Relationships with Eastern Europe) have led to several dialogues in this country. A principal Communist thinker involved in

U.S. dialogues has been Herbert Aptheker, author of *The Urgency of Marxist-Christian Dialogue* (1970).

Guidelines for Dialogue

There are several questions which have to be addressed in considering serious dialogue: Is it desirable? Is it possible? What are the objectives? Let's look at each of these questions in an effort to note those conditions which are essential to meaningful dialogue.

Is dialogue desirable?   One important factor in answering this question is whether both sides see the need of dialogue and recognize it as desirable. Thus far greater interest has been shown by Christians than Marxists, who are subject to charges of "revisionism" should they be willing to engage in serious dialogue. But certainly people who are concerned for the future of this world must see as desirable every effort at communication and enhancement of understanding between opposing forces. Christianity and Marxism are deeply embedded in the ideological struggle between East and West. Because this struggle appears to be a dominant factor in determining the course of our civilization, we all have a stake in the quest for greater understanding and the discovery of areas in which mutual cooperation and support may be possible.

Is dialogue possible?   There are many questions that arise here. The rigidly orthodox on each side would maintain that the differences are too great, the gap too wide, for any possibility of meaningful dialogue. Such groups resist dialogue because its success is equated with "selling out" to the enemy. Yet, as most participants in these dialogues would acknowledge, the indispensable prerequisite for successful dialogue is fidelity to one's own tradition; without this integrity the dialogue cannot be fruitful.

For the dialogue to be seen as possible, there must be the conviction that truth can be found *together,* no matter how contradictory each starting point may be. There must be the willingness to be open, to recognize the humanity of those on the other side, to put the best construction on what they say, and to acknowledge that they also have a share of the truth. Dialogue is possible when a sense of confidence and freedom is present in regard to one's own tradition. Signs of this freedom emerged among European Marxists in the 1960s, encouraging the possibility of fruitful dialogue.

One reason often given for the impossibility of dialogue with communists was the totalitarianism of communist regimes, marked by the imprisonment and torture of political opponents, mass executions, persecution of Christians and other religious minorities, etc. Engaging in dialogue does not mean we ignore such activity, to say nothing of condoning it. In part, it may be the result of unscrupulous people acquiring absolute power in a totalitarian system, as in the case of Stalin. But there is also the problem posed for any group which claims an absolute truth and seeks to realize it in a world that is resistant to its truth. This kind of situation is one in which both Christians and Communists have found themselves, and both groups have succumbed at times to the temptation of imposing their truth upon unwilling subjects. A Christian from England who has been involved in dialogue makes this point in a forceful manner:

> There is hardly a crime that can be attributed to Communists which they have not learned from Christians. Heresy hunts, persecution, censorship, inquisition, brainwashing, violence—the church has been, and still is in parts of the world, author of or party to them all [5]

While it is true that Christian resources for self-criticism have always counteracted the church's misuse of power, it is nonetheless well for us to remember that no one sits down to talk with completely clean hands.

What are the objectives of dialogue?   We have already indicated that understanding and mutual cooperation are objectives that we would hope to see realized at least to some degree through dialogue. To engage in dialogue is always to affirm our common humanity, for it indicates our acceptance of each other by taking each other seriously, regardless of how far apart we may be in our fundamental commitments. This activity can help to create an atmosphere in which communication is encouraged on various levels between East and West. To quote the Czech theologian, Jan Lochman: "The need to reflect and to exchange one's thought with the other side is more than the private concern of the notorious intellectuals: it is a vital concern of every healthy society. . . ."[6]

Common Themes of Dialogue

A principal factor in generating interest in dialogue was the discovery of the "young Marx." As was noted previously, Marx's early writings clearly display a basic humanistic and idealistic motivation. This humanistic concern has interested Christian thinkers and has given a lively impetus to Marxist studies among Marxists themselves. Thus one theme in the dialogue has been a comparison of Christian and Marxist humanism. It has provided a common ground and has opened the way on each side to appreciate those aspirations and ideals which motivate the other side.

While the subject of humanism reveals a common concern to fashion a world in which the human being can live a truly liberated and fulfilled life, that subject also raises the fundamental religious issue between Marxism and Christianity. The humanism of Marx is atheistic, while the Christian believes that humanism truly flowers were human beings recognize their creaturehood under a holy and loving God. Here Christians have been reminded of Marx's perception of the church at his time—a perception which unfortunately was largely accurate. He saw in those who believed in God a reactionary community, insensitive to the oppressive evils of an industrial society. Marx's conclusion was that God is an idea which justifies the status quo and stands in the way of those changes which would bring about a more humane society. In order for us to become truly human, God must die. Thus Marx's denial of God is a necessary correlate of his desire to exalt the human. The point is eloquently made by the Marxist, Roger Garaudy:

> Our own task as Communists is to draw near to man in his most glorious dreams and his most sublime hopes, to draw near to him in a real and practical way, so that Christians themselves might find here on our earth a beginning of their heaven.[7]

The concern of Christians in dialogue on this issue has been not to respond defensively, but to be willing to be instructed by the valid insights of Marx. Too often we have placed God in heaven, remote from the dynamics of history. Too often we have restricted our relation to God to the prayer closet, or the house of worship. The meaning of salvation has often been limited to the individual in his private relation to God. More recently we have begun to appreciate and emphasize the fact that salvation is a corporate concept. It is the coming of the kingdom which unites us with our sisters and brothers in Christ. We are saved not only *from* something—our sinful selves and all that that implies— we are saved *to* something. The new life in Christ begins now and brings with it responsibility for the world. If this consciousness had been moving the church of Marx's time, he would at least have had to come to terms with an authentic Christian humanism. His idea that religion is simply "the opium of the people" would have been challenged by a divine discontent among many Christians with injustice and oppression.

Another subject that has interested Christians and Marxists in dialogue is their respective understandings of alienation, or what Christians call "sin." The Marxist contention that private ownership of property is the root of the human problem is clearly simplistic to Christians. Yet the

Marxist analysis of alienation in the capitalistic society can be quite instructive for Christians in understanding the dehumanizing features of life lived under a highly competitive economic system. Alienation is a recurring theme throughout Marx's work, reflecting his concern over the unfulfilled character of human existence.

Another theme which has been pursued is the character of hope in Marxism and Christianity. Both maintain an *eschaton,* and end toward which history is moving. For Christians that end is a consummation created by God in his sovereignty, while for Marxists the fulfillment of human history will be the creation of a classless society by fully autonomous and free human beings. This theme as well as many others reveals a fact often noted by Christians, that Marxism can only be understood as a creature of the Christian tradition. It arose in opposition to that tradition, but it also has been nurtured and shaped by it. It is a modern-day "Christian heresy," a secularized version of the Christian message.

There are, of course, many other themes which have been pursued, too numerous to mention here. But it is well for us to recognize that whatever the obstacles to a genuine meeting of the minds between Christians and Marxists, there are some powerful ideals at work in both traditions—ideals which affirm human solidarity and justice. As Christians living in the affluent West we are compelled to recognize that the very appeal and attractiveness of Marxist communism is enhanced by the sense of purposelessness and lack of moral direction that presently pervade the Western world. Marxism gives a vision and a hope to people who are oppressed, just at the time when we in the West are experiencing a cultural and moral malaise. We are afflicted by relativism, where people no longer recognize a common good, but see only their own private good in competition with the values and desires of everyone else. We do not seem to be capable of exercising moral leadership in the world because we are perceived to have one overriding goal: creating more wealth for ourselves in a world in which the rich become richer and the poor become poorer. It is a time for profound self-examination on the part of the church and every Christian. The dialogue with Marxists should indeed help us to discover just who we are as Christians and just what we ought to be doing as stewards in the world God has given us.

8 Marxist Humanism and the Hope of the Gospel

by James M. Childs Jr.

One of the most important and widely discussed developments in contemporary theology is the movement called the "theology of hope." This school of thought takes its name from the book *Theology of Hope* written by one of its leading theologians, Jürgen Moltmann of the University of Tübingen. Equally influential is Wolfhart Pannenberg and prominent in Roman Catholic circles is Johann Baptist Metz. Although the roots and concerns of hope theology are manifold and its proponents differ among themselves, all three of the theologians named have been significantly shaped by their dialogue and its ramifications for Christian-Marxist interchange and for theology that is the subject of this chapter.

Ernst Bloch: Marxist and Philosopher of Hope

Professor Jan Lochman has referred to Ernst Bloch as "one of the patriarchs of nonconformist Marxist thinkers." The truth of this judgment is evident in his work and punctuated by the events of his life. In contrast to Marxism in general, Bloch's thought is in constant dialogue with the Judaeo-Christian tradition. Bloch loves the Bible. His work is filled with discussion of the prophetic and apocalyptic elements of the biblical traditions and with the New Testament promise of the kingdom of God in the preaching of Jesus. In addition, he has been deeply affected by the mysticism and messianism of such heterodox Christian thinkers as Montanus, Marcion, Joachim of Flores, and Thomas Müntzer. Beyond these affinities with Christian tradition, which have stimulated so much dialogue with contemporary theologians, Bloch's brand of Marxism also displays the influence of idealist philosophy, existentialism, and ancient Neo-Platonism. These dimensions of his thought have also served to set him apart from the mainstream of orthodox Marxism.

Born in Germany in 1885, Bloch launched his career at the University of Leipzig in 1918 with the publication of *Von Geist der Utopie* (The Spirit of Utopia). This work was followed closely by the publication of a study of the "left-wing" 16th-century Anabaptist reformer, Thomas Müntzer, known for his advocacy of a simple, godly, communistic society, which he realized briefly in the community at Mülhausen in Germany. Bloch's ideas came to fullest expression in his major work, *Das Prinzip Hoffnung* (The Principle of Hope), written in the United States between 1938 and 1947. After World War II, Bloch returned to East Germany and taught again at Leipzig until his retirement in 1957. During this time he became editor of a controversial journal, some of whose editors and collaborators were arrested and imprisoned. Bloch himself was not well received by Communist party officials. From 1957 to 1959 his works were condemned, and he was forbidden to publish. Finally, in 1961 he gained political asylum in West Germany and finished his career there as professor at the University of Tübingen.

Although Bloch is atypical as a Marxist, he is a Marxist nonetheless and represents a legitimate development of Marx's thought. Certainly he shares Marx's view that revolutionary action is required to overturn the economic, political, and theological hierarchies of capitalism that are responsible for social inequities and the human alienation of class exploitation.[1] In short, Bloch shares Marx's socialist vision of a classless society. The following affirmation from Bloch illustrates this point.

> *Only Marxism has produced the theory and practice for a better world,*
> not in order to abrogate the present one, as in most abstract social utopias,
> but in oder to transform this world economically and dialectically.[2]

More specifically, it is Marx's humanism that he wishes to develop and lift up. This humanism is associated by many primarily with Marx's early works. Bloch believes, however, that the human ideal has always been the guide and standard even in the later writings. "Marxism . . . has been since its inception 'humanity in action,' the human countenance coming to fulfillment."[3] Thus it is the humanistic note that sounds the loudest as Bloch echoes Marx's critique of capitalism:

> . . . the alienation, dehumanization, and objectification, the transformation of all people and things into commodities, which capitalism increasingly has brought about, comprise for Marx the ancient enemy which in capitalism as capitalism has finally achieved a victory beyond anything in the past. Certainly humanism is the born enemy of this dehumanization. Indeed, since Marxism is essentially only this struggle against the dehumanization which reaches its acme in capitalism (until the latter is utterly transcended), it follows . . . that true Marxism, in its dynamics of the class struggle, and in its substantive goal is, and must be, humanism and humanitarianism enhanced.[4]

Yet Bloch goes beyond Marx in his own humanist philosophy. Indeed, he is critical of Marx for making the economy, rather than human consciousness, the fundamental determinant of human history. Such a view shortchanges the human spirit as the shaper of its own destiny. Therefore, Bloch replies to Marx:

> Man does not live by bread alone. Outward things, no matter how extensive their importance and our need to attend to them, are merely suggestive, not creative. People, not things and not the mighty course of events outside ourselves (which Marx falsely places above us), write history. His [Marx's] determinism applies to the economic future, to the necessary economic-institutional change; but the new man, the leap, the power of love and light, and morality itself are not yet accorded the requisite independence in the definitive social order.[5]

For Ernst Bloch, Marx focused too much on criticizing the capitalist economic system itself. He did not pay sufficient attention to the antihuman forces of oppression which are there in the heart of humankind and which are more fundamental than the economic order. Marx made a good case against capitalist economy, but the fulfillment of the human spirit which Marx's revolution was to make room for is still missing.[6] Even the success of an economic revolution is not adequate to still fundamental human questioning about our reason for existence when, ". . . despite a plentiful supply of daily bread, the other bread of life, the concrete 'What'of What-for and Where-to begins to dwindle.'"[7]

In the mind and heart of Ernst Bloch the fulfillment of the human spirit, the key to our reason for existence and our hope for existence is to be found in his vision of utopia. Bloch's utopia is the nonviolent, classless "Kingdom of Freedom," which he portrays for us in his philosophy of hope.

Bloch's philosophy of hope is a philosophy of the "not-yet." Reality is seen as a sea of possibilities; it is open to the advent of the new. Indeed, we should not view reality merely as a chain of events in which the past determines the present and the future is but an outgrowth of both. To see the world that way is a *hopeless* form of mechanical determinism in which all our efforts are for naught. As Bloch puts it colorfully:

> If the world were basically only a mechanism . . . then history would be like trout fighting or making love in a tank whilst the cook without is already advancing from the door, bearing with her the knife disparate to, yet desctructive of, the whole process in the tank.[8]

Rather, a philosophy of hope, a philosophy of the not-yet future, understands reality from a perspective which expects the radically new and unpredictable to break in from the future of possibility. The future is like an open space that creatively draws the present to itself. In a philosophy of hope one does not simply look at life cynically and with resignation. Even the grim record of human behavior cannot dampen our hope in the possibilities of the future.

Bloch's explanation of reality in terms of the power of the future to create new possibilities is directly related to the phenomenon of *hope* which is part of the makeup of humanity. Our daydreams, our will to utopia, our sense of anticipation and expectation, our longing for a better world for humankind; all these are evidence of humanity's orientation to the future. This is an outlook that often finds expression in the drive toward revolutionary change. However, this drive is a drive toward a genuinely *new* life, not simply toward renewal or reform. Bloch makes that clear:

> A clear distinction must be made between renewal and the new life. For renewal implies recourse to what has been . . . whereas the new life implies advance toward what has yet never appeared.[9]

This vision of hope or philosophy of the future certainly has some roots in Marx's thought. Bloch credits Marx with introducing the idea of a future that is open to change and new possibility. With Marx, in contrast to the thought that preceded him, knowledge is no longer confined to the past, what has already happened, but is now also oriented to the future. In the dialectics of Marx's thought, the world is capable of transformation to a new future and reality must be understood in terms of this not-yet possibility.[10]

However, for all that can be said about the formative influence of Marx, it seems that it is the Bible that has fueled Bloch's imagination and stimulated his hope. Bloch states that the ". . . hope that we find in humanism came into the world in only one form—that of the Bible."[11] The hope of the messianic age, the hope of the kingdom, the promise of the future in the prophets and in Jesus, these are the focus of Bloch's passionate appreciation of the biblical traditions. This eschatological preaching and expectation of God's future new age is for Bloch the dominant and overriding motif in the Bible. Certainly, Bloch believes Jesus is thoroughly dominated by his expectation of the imminent coming of the kingdom of God:

> With Jesus, eschatological preaching has primacy over moral preaching and determines it. Not only the money changers will be driven from the temple with a whip, as they were by Jesus; the whole state and temple will be brought down by a catastrophe, most thoroughly and in short order. The great eschatological chapter (Mark 13) is one of the best-attested in the New Testament; without this utopia, the Sermon on the Mount cannot be understood at all.[12]

Bloch follows many contemporary biblical scholars in the opinion that Jesus' expectation of the imminent end affected his ethical teaching. There is no reflection on economic questions, there is no call for political revolution, and there is no systematic discussion of the just state. Still, Bloch insists, Jesus did not compromise with the existing political oppression; he did not give up his proclamation of a "new aeon"; and he founded a new social community in early Christianity marked by a love communism and an identification with the poor.[13] Though the Bible sketches no clear portrait of utopia, Jesus and his early followers show us the path along which it lies. Later Christian accounts which identify the kingdom with the church, some form of the state, or with a primarily otherworldly hope are, in Bloch's view, a distortion of both the New Testament witness and the prophetic hope. Bloch's admiration for Jesus is evident everywhere.

Ernst Bloch's credentials as an atheist, however, are still very much in order. Bloch's love of the Bible is rooted in its vision of the coming kingdom interpreted as a humanistic vision of the overcoming of oppression and the establishment of a utopia of human fulfillment. So he wrote in *The Principle of Hope*, "God appears therefore as the hypostasized ideal of the as yet truly undeveloped essence of man; he appears as Utopian entelechy (actuality)." Therefore, to do justice to the Bible's message for Marxist humanism we need to ''de-theocratize'' it or de-divinize it. That is, we need to free the biblical message of liberation for the poor and oppressed from the oppressive message of an almighty, transcendent God who stands over us and rules from above. Then the riches of the Bible imagery for the hope of human fulfillment in a human ''kingdom of freedom'' can be mined and put to use. The kingdom of freedom is Bloch's humanistic translation of the biblical promise of the kingdom of God. It is an atheistic revision of the biblical story told in human terms. The hope for a human kingdom of freedom, Bloch says, ''is what lives on when the opium, the fool's paradise of the Other-world, has been burnt away to ashes.That remains as a call signaling the way to the fulfilled This-world of a new earth.''[14]

The Theology of Hope: Theologians in Dialogue with Bloch

The theologians who have been identified with the term ''theology of hope,'' principally Jürgen Moltmann and Wolfhart Pannenberg, have presented us with complex theologies. They have attempted to gather up the insights of modern biblical, theological, and scientific scholarship and bring them into correlation with both the tradition of the catholic faith and contemporary visions of reality. They have been attempting to address the problems that theology has created for itself as well as the problems the modern world has created for theology. As such, their works involve discussion with the history of Christian thought on virtually all major topics of Christian doctrine, interaction with philosophical and theological developments, especially in the 19th and 20th centuries, appropriation of the peculiar insights of contemporary biblical scholarship, and reaction to the claims of both the physical and human sciences. With such an extensive agenda, it is obvious that the few remarks which follow cannot do full justice to the work of these theologians. We can only concentrate on a few prominent points of intersection with the Marxism of Ernst Bloch. However, in so doing, we will be able to lift up some of the most important themes of hope theology and also discover one paradigm for Christian-Marxist encounter.

The history of Christian theology is a history of dialogue with various philosophies. Augustine's involvement with Neo-Platonism and Thomas Aquinas' use of Aristotle are classic examples. Recent theology has interacted with existentialism, the process philosophy of Alfred North Whitehead and current philosophical analysis of the meaning of language. These are but a few examples which make the point. The dialogue between theology and philosophy is both necessary and risky. Theology always expresses itself in terms of the culture it is addressing. The influence of the culture is simply unavoidable, and being responsive to culture is necessary for good communication. Philosophy is often both a shaper and an interpreter of the way a culture understands the world. A failure to engage philosophy can result in a failure to understand and speak clearly to the mind-set of an age. However, interaction with philosophy carries the other risk that philosophical ideas will dominate and distort theological truth. Thus, philosophy should provide a stimulus and a resource to theology so that theology does its own work better. Theology, then, must maintain its own integrity and a measure of critical distance from philosophy. There is every evidence that the theologians of hope have been both stimulated by Bloch's philosophy and critical of it.

Bloch the Stimulus

Walter Capps has made the following observation: "Without Ernst Bloch there would probably be no hope school. Or, if there were one, without Bloch, it would probably not be known. Without doubt, Bloch's writings . . . are the school's primary stimulus."[15] This is a bold claim, perhaps too bold, but there is no doubt that Bloch's thought has remarkable qualities to serve as a catalyst for the development we associate with hope theology.

The modern scientific view of our world tells us that it is a world of *process*. Far from being an unchanging order of creation or simply a fallen, sinful world with no hope but destruction, the world of today's consciousness is evolving, moving, developing. Obviously, when we think of reality as process rather than being a more or less static order, history and the future become more prominent concerns. Marxism with its idea of historical process moving toward the achievement of the classless society is well suited to this new climate of thought and is, indeed, a product of it. From the Marxist perspective, adherence to capitalist structures of class is seen as a conservative attempt to hold back the course of history's evolution toward the classless society. The alleged hierarchy of power and privilege in capitalism are pictured as a reflection of the old static world view of the Middle Ages which saw creation as ordered in a fixed hierarchy of being. At the same time, acceptance of the injustices and oppression of a class society can readily be interpreted as resignation to a sinful and imperfect world that can't be changed, a vale of tears that is passing away.

The question of history and the future was largely neglected by Christian theology in the mid-20th century. This is evident in the treatment of eschatology, the doctrine of the end times, often associated with the teaching of the coming kingdom of God. For traditional theology the doctrine of the end times is finally otherworldly talk about heaven in eternity. Eschatology did not treat the question of the future of this historical existence but concentrated on the promise of eternity for saved individuals above and beyond history. In fact, eschatology receded from view as an important theme and was overshadowed by this concentration on the promise of heaven to each individual believer.

Liberal theology in the 20th century, though breaking the traditional mold in many ways, was hardly different in its emphasis on the spiritual life of the individual to the neglect of the kingdom theme which pointed to the future of world history. Rudolf Bultmann, for example, the controversial but highly influential biblical scholar, interpreted the New Testament as having nothing to say about the history of the world and its future hope. Rather he taught that the basic message of the gospel pertained simply to the internal life of the individual. Biblical hope for the eschatological kingdom of God was spiritualized in terms of personal faith life and removed from the arena of history. In short, much of both traditional and mid-20th century theology tended to be otherworldly and/or individualistic in interpreting the faith. All of this stood in contrast to the general impulses of modern thought and the specific thrust of Marxist thought. At the same time, however, contemporary biblical studies were rediscovering the centrality of eschatology in the Bible. That is, the Bible's message is future-oriented; it constantly points us in the direction of God's intention for the history of his creation. In the New Testament this is voiced in terms of Jesus' central proclamation: the coming of the kingdom of God. Thus the Bible is a book involved with the theme of hope in expectation of the new future that God will bring to pass. It is the convergence of these developments of biblical scholarship with Ernst Bloch's biblically influenced Marxist philosophy of hope which has proven a stimulus to theologians of hope. Carl Braaten, a Lutheran theologian and the most prominent American to be associated with the school of hope theology, has stated that Bloch's philosophy has ". . . had the effect of arousing the systematic imagination to unite with Old Testament studies and to reassert a fundamental continuity between the Old and New Testaments in terms of an eschatological interpretation of hope and history, promise and future."[16] Thus the theologians of hope see in the biblical traditions a point of contact with our contemporary concern for history and the future and with our experience of hope, which Bloch has elaborated in his discussion of the human longing for utopia.

The biblical hope, the vision of the future kingdom that God will bring in, pervades the message of the prophets, the apocalyptic visionaries, and the New Testament. It is a hope for the individual, to be sure, but it is, more fundamentally, a promise and hope for the universal future of humankind, of history. Moltmann is worth quoting at length on this point:

> Christian theology speaks of God *historically*. It speaks of "the God of Abraham, Isaac, and Jacob," and it speaks of "the Father of Jesus Christ." It connects talk about God with remembrance of *historical persons*. Christian theology speaks of "the God of the exodus" as in the First Commandment and of "the God who raised Jesus from the dead," as in the Easter gospel. It combines belief in God with remembrance of these *historical events* and *root experiences*.
>
> But Christian theology speaks of this history *eschatologically*. That is, it proclaims the "God of Abraham" as the God of the promise of blessing for *all* people. It expects from the God of the exodus a future in which *all* lands will be full of his majesty and beauty. It proclaims the "Father of Jesus Christ" as the *one* God of *all* men and his coming kingdom as the liberation of the whole groaning creation from its misery. This is what is special and unique in the biblical message about God. It is not a metaphysics of the highest being, but it emerges from history and has the future and the end of history, that is liberation, as its goal. It is a belief in God, which is harnessed between memory and hope. Therefore, this language about God cannot be abstract and without a history, but it must be a concrete and liberating language. By awakening hope in the coming of God through remembrance of history, it inaugurates a new history and new freedom for men.[17]

From this vantage point, then, we see God as the God of history, the coming one who will bring in the new. God is "the power of the future" (Pannenberg). The focus has shifted away from God as "up there," above and beyond us in the eternal heaven that we covet as our destiny.

The Critique of Bloch

Points of convergence between Bloch's thought and the theology of hope are evident even in these few remarks. Though Bloch has provided a stimulus to theology, however, he has also been the object of its criticism. Wolfhart Pannenberg pays tribute to Bloch for giving theology the courage to recover the central "theme of eschatology in the biblical traditions.'' He acknowledges the power of Bloch's vision of a still-open future to which we reach out in anticipation of the radically new utopia.[18] At the same time, Pannenberg is quick to point out that Bloch's expectation of a new utopian future collapses under its own weight without the idea of God bringing in that future. Bloch's purely human-istic formula for the hope of a new future is ultimately hope-*less* for there is no ''power of the future'' to bring in the kingdom. Instead, Bloch must rely on the potencies he discerns in the wishes and longings of human beings as providing a basis for hope in the future. However, this is not hope in a coming future; it is simply hope concerning how people feel about the future. Such a hope is undermined by the fact that people become self-satisfied with their present.[19] And, one might add, a hope built on potencies and possibilities that reside in humanity itself must bear the weight of history which simply displays the fact that the best of hopes for the human future have always been frustrated by humankind itself.

Although Jürgen Moltmann sees profound benefits for theology in taking seriously the critique of Bloch's atheism, he also argues that Bloch's atheism cannot sustain his hope. Specifically, Bloch has not dealt adequately with the problem of death.

> All utopias of the kingdom of God or of man, all hopeful pictures of the happy life, all revolutions of the future, remain hanging in the air and bear within them the germ of boredom and decay—and for that reason also adopt a militant and extortionate attitude to life—as long as there is no certainty in the face of death and no hope which carries love beyond death.[20]

Marxism stands silent before the problem of death. Bloch himself at-tempts to deal with it by a revival of the ancient Platonic doctrine of the immortality and transmigration of souls.[21] However, in the final analysis, this is an avoidance of the reality of death, a dismissal of the problem.

By contrast, the theology of hope takes the reality of death seriously in the reality of the crucifixion. Hope is grounded, then, in the triumph of the resurrection, which is not the denial of death but its defeat. It is the resurrection which reveals in the present the promise and substance of the future kingdom of God. The hopes and dreams of human longing for a better future are ''hopes'' and ''dreams'' because of the evil of the present. The crucifixion mirrors this situation powerfully. The res-urrection provides the ground of the future on which hope can stand.

Political Theology

The impetus to the recovery of eschatology, which Ernst Bloch has provided for theology, has had profound implications for the development of a political theology. One of the characteristics of traditional and modern theologies which stress the faith and destiny of the individual at the expense of eschatological hope for the future of history is a tendency toward producing quietism, that is, a religiously motivated lack of involvement with justice issues or social concerns. Instead the mission of the gospel is understood as focused primarily on the private faith of individuals. The theology of hope, though certainly not the only theology to do so, has challenged this quietism.

In his *Theology of the World,* Johannes Metz introduces the notion of a *political theology* and declares that, ''The deprivatizing of theology is the primary critical task of political theology.''[22] Otherwise, Metz says, there is a danger of reducing the eschatological proclamation of God's salvation to the small scale of the personal and private decisions.[23] In this instance Metz is targeting recent theologies of an existential, personalist orientation which make no connection between the Christian faith and life and the concerns of world history and the political sphere. By contrast, Metz echoes Bloch's thought and other theologians of hope in saying that, ''God is no longer merely 'above' history, he is himself in it, in that he is also constantly 'in front of it' as its free, uncontrolled future. . . . He is of decisive importance for the reality of history itself.''[24] In the biblical traditions God's eschatological promises for the future of history are freedom, peace, justice, and reconciliation. These promises force a new sense of social responsibility on the church. Speaking out of the Christian conscience the church becomes the source of ''a liberating critique'' of social and political reality and planning. Because the eschatological promises are *eschatological* no social achievement short of the kingdom of God can be identified with achievement of the promises. Nonetheless, in the spirit of hope, the church engages in critical involvement with all societies, spurred on by the kingdom's promises.[25]

In a similar vein Wolfhart Pannenberg is critical of the ''other worldly distortion'' of traditional eschatologies. Such traditional hopes are escapist in nature, a pious longing for individual communion with a God understood to be above and apart from the world. In contrast, the eschatological perspective relates God directly to our world as its future in the coming of the kingdom. God is the God who is coming to transform the world through his rule. Thus one can hardly wish to leave or escape the world for the sake of God. Rather, one is *converted to the world*. Love affirms God's world by actively seeking its transformation.[26]

Jürgen Moltmann also calls for a political theology that lifts up the political dimensions of the promise of the future kingdom of God which is so central to the Christian faith and message.[27] As we have seen, he echoes Bloch's concern for justice and relief of the oppressed in this world. However, he does so with a difference. The difference is that the task of liberation can be undertaken as meaningful and filled with hope only in view of God's justifying grace and resurrection promise.

> The gospel of the kingdom and of the justice of God in Christ can enter into a cooperative endeavor with social-revolutionary work for "those who labor and are heavily laden" and political work for "those who are humiliated and offended," precisely because it goes beyond this in promising justification of the sinner and the resurrection of the dead. In so doing it can destroy the seeds of resignation which spring up in the course of social-political work and it can itself become a stimulus to creative imagination.[28]

Concluding Thoughts

The interchange between the theologians of hope and the thought of Ernst Bloch is one model for the dialogue between Christianity and Marxism. It is marked by a mixture of appreciation and criticism. These theologians are open to being stimulated and instructed by Bloch but, at the same time, they know who they are as Christians and they seek to maintain the integrity of the gospel in the face of all challenges from the side of Marxist humanism.

In the final analysis, though interpretation of the Bible is a prominent feature of this interaction, it is two features of the Marxist outlook in general that emerge as most significant. The first of these is the Marxist attitude toward history and the future. For Marx's thought there is both severe criticism of the failures of history and confidence in the openness to change. For the theologians of hope there is the relentless testimony of the cross against the failures of history and, now, there is the rediscovery of its openness to transformation in the promise of the kingdom of God. The second thrust is Marx's emphasis on *praxis,* the active pursuit of changing the world—not merely explaining it or theorizing about it. For theologians of hope the renewed sense of history from the perspective of eschatological promise has produced a political theology, a new praxis of social action conceived as integral to the gospel mission of the church.

Some Christian thinkers, however, regard the theologians of hope as far too theoretical. They are open to the charge of playing intellectual games with one atypical Marxist. The fact that Pannenberg has repudiated Marxist political philosophy and the others seem ambivalent about it serves to reinforce the suspicion. In view of some current theologies of liberation, discussed in the next chapter, one has to admit that the theology of hope occupies the middle ground between repudiation of Marxism and some of its more appreciative Christian proponents.

9 Marxism and Latin American Liberation Theology

by Marc Kolden

"Liberation theology" is the name given to the theology which emerged during the 1970s in Latin America; it makes explicit use of Marxist thought. This theology arises from a concern to understand the meaning of the biblical message and to construct a position about the church's mission in a situation of great economic and political oppression. Liberation theology also takes seriously the positive contributions of Marxism as seen in the socialism of Allende's Chile and the communism of Castro's Cuba. *Liberation* is this theology's term to connect the biblical idea of the deliverance of those who are in bondage or suffering and the Marxist hope for freedom from class oppression.

Marxist revolutionary movements for political liberation helped reveal to Latin American theologians the ways in which their countries' poverty and dependence are bound up with economic and political domination by North Atlantic nations. In these liberation struggles, in which the churches often have been found to be in support of totalitarian regimes and of an unjust status quo, the discrepancy between the official theology, which has encouraged such actions by the churches, and the biblical emphases on justice and freedom became obvious. Thus it was necessary to reconstruct theology to make the churches' teachings and practices correspond with their beliefs.

Some theologians have been directly involved in political movements for liberation and others have worked primarily to enhance their churches' identification with oppressed people, thereby building up a more powerful base for liberation. Majority Roman Catholic theologians as well as many mainline Protestants have made common cause in this effort, often despite considerable governmental and ecclesiastical pressure to cease working for social change.

The Main Ideas of Liberation Theology

Despite the obvious influence of the contemporary situation, liberation theology is not something entirely new. It is very old—at least in its major themes. The central Old Testament message of the exodus, the social pronouncements of the great Israelite prophets Amos, Isaiah, and Jeremiah, and the teachings of Jesus, especially in the gospels of Matthew and Luke, provide ample grounding for this theology's concerns. Yet the uses to which these themes are put are new, for they challenge the ways in which Christians have so often domesticated the biblical cries for peace and justice and have made liberation into something which is possible only in heaven.

The contribution of Marxism may be seen above all in liberation theology's *critical stance* toward both society and previous theological positions. Liberation theologians consider much traditional theology to be ideology, offering a religious rationale for the self-interest of dominant groups as well as an "explanation" which legitimizes the present suffering of the oppressed by promising hope only for another world. For example, if we interpret Jesus' words about the poor being blessed or the captives being liberated as having only a "spiritual" meaning—referring to inward poverty or liberation from personal sin—this is an instance of theology's ideological function.

Marx's insight that "the ruling ideas are the ideas of the ruling class" is cited to point out how no theological system is "pure" or completely objective. All theology is conditioned by the status and concerns of the theologians and churches. While we in North America often call their theology "Latin American" theology and ours simple "theology," it might be more accurate to speak of our theology as "capitalist" theology or "affluent" theology (or white or male theology). This would help us to be more self-critical and aware of the ways in which nontheological factors such as position or wealth affect our thinking. In appropriating this critical approach from Marx, liberation theologians are taking a stance much like the Old Testament prophets in their denunciations of the ways in which religion was used by priests to support unjust kings (see Jer. 5:31).

A second major theme of liberation theologians is the emphasis that the purpose of the Christian faith is to *transform the world*. Again, they use familiar biblical teachings about justice and righteousness, but they do not hold them to refer only to the heavenly realm or to the inner life but especially to the socio-political realm. In an often-cited passage, they stress how the very word "to know" God means "to do justice" (Jer. 22:16). This same connotation is present in the New Testament as well, where Jesus' followers are called his "disciples," meaning both that they learn from Jesus and follow after him. There is no true knowledge of Jesus which does not result in patterning one's life after his in a world-transforming direction.

Many liberation theologians have had the experience that seeking reform within unjust political systems of Latin America does not work; the systems themselves have to be changed. Thus acts of charity or benevolence or personal kindness, though well intended, are not sufficient for Christian obedience. Love on a social scale means justice, in the sense of fairness, and this may demand radical changes if the system of property ownership or production or governance prevents justice from being achieved. In such situations, "revolutionary activity is not an intrusion in the world; it is a response to reality and, in turn, it moves the world towards its realization."[1]

It is necessary to make a point here about their understanding of violence, since many critics of liberation theology reject it simply because it seems to promote violence and revolution. The liberation theologians reply that such criticism fails to see the violence already present in unjust systems. This is the violence by which a few oppress many and where being in favor of "law and order" actually encourages massive, continuing, "legal" violence against all who are not in power. Here revolution could be justified (as it was in the American Revolution of 1776, for example) as a way of ending the built-in violence of an inherently unjust system. In all such struggles, Christians will need to be guided in their actions by seeking the good of the "neighbor" (that is, those in need) and not primarily their own good. Christians will also be critical of many revolutionary movements which simply replace one unjust system with another. This is all the more reason, liberation theologians argue, for Christians to be involved in liberation struggles.

A third theme which occurs frequently is the *distinction between "development" and "liberation."* We in the wealthy North Atlantic nations, who have benefited economically by the industrial and technological growth of the past two centuries, often consider our countries to have "developed." We look at poor nations and judge that they are *under*developed; if they had expertise and aid from us they too could be developed. The fallacy in this, as Marxists and liberation theologians point out, is that the wealthy nations progressed at the expense of the poorer nations, exploiting both their natural resources and low-cost labor (in colonialism and with slavery). If development depends on such imbalance, then there is no way any longer that poor nations can develop while we in the wealthy nations still maintain our standard of living.

A more accurate way to evaluate the situation would be to see that there are poor nations *because* there are rich nations—to see that "underdevelopment" is caused by the "developed" nations. The basic problem of the poor nations is *dependence* on and domination by the rich nations. And if that is the problem, "development" within the present world economic structure will not be a solution. The cure for dependence is *liberation*—freedom from the present system within a new system. Liberation theologians take this analysis farther than either Marxist or capitalist thinkers because they assert that neither the problem nor the solution can be understood in purely economic terms, because human well-being is not to be defined merely in terms of material standard of living. The biblical understanding of *shalom* (peace, justice, wholeness) gives a more adequate content to liberation; it includes material well-being but also communal, racial, and sexual justice.

If one accepts the distinction between development and liberation, then it is clear that the liberation approach reveals that conflict is inevitable because justice can be achieved only by extensive changes which will not allow present oppressor groups to continue in their ways. This conclusion follows not only from Marxist analysis but also from the way in which the God of the Bible is seen to use groups and movements to bring judgment on those who serve themselves rather than God and the people.

From this it may be claimed that *the God of the Bible takes sides*. Already in the exodus, God is said to side with the slaves against Pharaoh; and the message of the prophets is always on behalf of the poor and against the rich, powerful, and privileged. So too, when God sends Jesus, he comes (see especially Luke 4) to bring good news to the poor, release to the captives, sight to the blind, and liberation to the oppressed. And, as Chapter 1 of Luke's gospel notes, this will involve "putting down the mighty from their seats."

Some people reject this emphasis on God siding with the poor on the basis that God favors only the righteous poor or those who trust in him rather than the poor in general. Besides having to ignore a great amount of biblical evidence, this criticism usually has to reinterpret "poor" to mean "poor in spirit" and "bondage" to mean an inner slavery to sin— in this way getting around the plain meaning of such passages. Liberation theologians point out how such criticism functions as a rationalization for possessing wealth, power, and privilege and ignores both the inequities in the world and the call of Jesus to be with the poor— to give up what one has for their benefit and to follow him (see Mark 10).

Liberation theologians claim that the poor have an "edge" in understanding Scripture. To the poor the news of God's taking sides is good news and speaks directly to their situation. To many of us in the wealthy nations such news is threatening and we seek to "interpret" it in some way so as to blunt its force.

The *meaning of salvation is broadened* in liberation theology. It includes not only eternal life after death but greater fullness of life here on earth. Liberation theologians criticize much traditional belief, which has made salvation overly individualistic and otherworldly. At times it sounds almost as if liberation theologians equate salvation with political liberation because they have stated their case for having salvation *include* economic and political liberation with such sharpness. They certainly have rejected any modern understandings which hold that salvation is possible for individuals in terms of "authentic existence" or "self-actualization" but which ignore the larger human community.

Salvation in Christ is linked to the whole creative work of God as its completion and fulfillment. Gustavo Gutiérrez, perhaps the leading liberation theologian, states that the saving work of Christ to liberate people from sin involves also liberation from all its consequences—for example, injustice, hatred, and oppression. Obviously, this does not happen by itself in the death and resurrection of Christ, but it is to happen through the transforming work of faithful human beings. Working creatively in the world is seen as participating in God's salvific process and being in communion with God. Any fulfillments within history will be partial but they will point toward the promised transformation; indeed, "the elimination of misery and exploitation is a sign of the coming Kingdom."[2] There will be an end to history as we know it, but it will be the fulfillment and not the annihilation of this life. Therefore what we do now is of great importance beause liberating actions are part of the fulfillment, just as the absence of love and justice is the epitome of sin. Liberation is necessarily political, though not only political.

Gutiérrez speaks of three interrelated "levels" of liberation: the political liberation of oppressed people, the deeper liberation of people in history by participation in the creative work of God who transforms people and structures, and the ultimate liberation from sin into complete communion with God. These are said to be three interdependent levels to a single process; we should neither overly-spiritualize liberation nor identify it only with meeting immediate political needs. Thus, while this broadened definition of salvation clearly has much in common with a Marxist understanding of historical fulfillment, it is also critical of Marxism's truncating of reality to include only the historical process.

Evaluating Liberation Theology

We must not forget the situation out of which liberation theology grows. It is one in which radical change seems to offer the only hope for perennially oppressed people. We must not simply reject it for being too concerned with revolutionary action. To do so, especially from a position of relative safety and comfort, would be irresponsible—both to the Bible's insistence on God's concern for justice and an end to oppression and poverty and to the liberation theologian's genuine attempt to serve Christ in their time and place. Their conclusions have not been reached carelessly; only after the failure of every other alternative and in the face of inhuman conditions have they discovered the "unsubstitutable relevance" of Marxist analysis (the words are by Miguez Bonino).[3]

The question that arises then is whether theology can use a Marxist analysis of society without also sharing in other Marxist ideas which are clearly at odds with Christian faith. While it seems possible to avoid the explicit atheism of Marxism in making use of its social analysis, there is the danger that Marx's emphasis on economic factors will serve to reduce the relevance of other factors, particularly the activity of God in history. A related point is Marx's emphasis on the inevitability of class conflict; from a Christian point of view it is inadequate to define reality in such a way as to see class conflict as the only operative force in history. In addition to God, Christians would claim that powers such as love and suffering are also influential in reality.

Liberation theologians are aware of such dangers and they clearly intend to be *Christian* theologians and not simply to give a religious rationale for a Marxist political program. They would add that all theology uses categories from some social context; no theology is neutral. A particular value of Marxism is its awareness of the way in which thought is defined by the social reality of the thinker—and hence its stress on thinking critically. Thus just as liberation theologians need to be concerned to keep from identifying Christianity with any particular movement or program, so also they remind those of us in different contexts that we must guard our theology against this as well.

Certain points often made about Marx may apply to liberation theology as well. Both are more concerned about the community than about the individual, and both would claim that authentic individuality is found only in community. Both see evil as primarily systemic rather than rooted in individuals, and both hold that the overcoming of evil is not primarily found in forgiveness or regeneration but in the transformation of the system. One might wish to give equal time to the sinfulness of the individual, to the extent that no system will ever be sinless nor will it ever be able to offer liberation from death. Liberation theologians know this, but they do not stress it. Finally, both Marxism and liberation theology share in the criticism of traditional religion for merely legitimizing injustice and inaction. They differ, of course, in seeing the importance of God and Christianity in the world's future, but they make a powerful case for showing us in the churches where we have fallen short.

The key point for evaluation is liberation theology's definition of theology: that it is critical reflection on liberating activity, aimed not merely at understanding the world but at transforming it in accord with the revelation in Christ. In this understanding of theology they are decisively influenced by Marx. This definition alters some of the criteria traditionally used for judging theological statements. For example, theologians have often asked two questions of a theological claim: whether it is true to the Bible and the creeds and whether it is coherent or intelligible in terms of other things people know. When theology is related so directly to activity (liberation), however, a third criterion becomes important: to what sort of action does a particular theological statement lead?

The danger is that liberating action becomes the *only* criterion for truth, as sometimes seems to be suggested. Then theology risks equating truth with human action and with quite specific political action. This may lose the paradoxical way in which the biblical understanding of the truth that liberates people is related to Christ on the cross, where power is seen in weakness, in love, and in losing oneself for another.

Liberation theologians sometimes are in danger here, perhaps because in order to get a hearing they must state their case so radically. Most of them know that finally the church cannot be unambiguously partisan and that no revolutionary movement can be completely identified with the kingdom of God. In any case, it will be important to see that the goals and directions for transforming the world are shaped by Christian and not only Marxist content.

The most far-reaching form of this criticism has to do with liberation theology's linking of the liberation which Christ brings with political liberation from oppression. When reality is defined in terms of two classes in conflict, and when God in Christ is identified through and through with the oppressed and their liberation, there is a potential problem—and it is not merely one for those of us in the wealthy nations. It is a different sort of problem. In Marxist thinking, from which liberation theology gets this understanding, God is said to be the invention of the oppressors to keep the oppressed down. The beginning of all social criticism for Marx was the criticism of religion because religion was seen as the primary way of legitimizing unjust conditions. Liberation for Marx involved getting rid of the projection of a God so that humans could gain control of their own destiny. Humans were seen by Marx to be their own gods and there were no limits other than human limits. If theology now seeks to introduce the Christian notion of God into a liberation framework, thus speaking of Creator and creature, Savior and disciple, this is a vastly different notion of liberation: as service, losing one's life, going the second mile, turning the other cheek, living with the ambiguity of being in the image of God but not being one's own God. The problem for liberation theology may be that its major focus for understanding reality (oppressor/oppressed or dependence/liberation) implies a liberation different from that of the God "in whose service is perfect freedom." Another way of making this criticism is to say that liberation theology's Marxist method threatens to undercut its biblical content, even though it is that method which has allowed its content to speak so powerfully in the present situation.

The strengths of liberation theology are its questioning, its criticism, its unmasking of so much Christian self-deception, and its recovery of the biblical demands for justice and righteousness. No evaluation should allow us to avoid those challenges. No criticism should allow us to ignore the important contribution of Marxist thought in this program. Liberation theology challenges all Christians to seek in one way or another to abolish injustice and to build a better society; and it claims that in this struggle we will come to know more deeply Christ our liberator. Theology will not be quite the same again.

10 The Black Church and Marxism

by Will L. Herzfeld

Preliminary Reflections

Black theologians James Cone and Cornel West are right when they say that historically, except for a few isolated instances, the Black church in the United States and Marxism are strangers to one another. Because Marxism is a philosophy and the Black church an institution, some may consider that the two cannot be compared. To a certain extent this is true.

The Black church in the United States always has had a progressive tradition and has played a vital role in the lives of African-Americans from the days of chattel slavery. It continues to play this role in the ongoing struggle for liberation. The pioneer black educator and activist W.E.B. DuBois noted this at the turn of the century. He pointed out that there was a church organization for every 60 black families, and that it had assumed functions that were otherwise suppressed by the dominant society. Amusements, what little economic activity there was, education, and all forms of social intercourse were centered around the church. Occasional failures of black ministers and denominations do not change the overall picture of the church's essential usefulness to the black community.

As one who was active in the civil rights movement of the 1960s, I am aware that since that turbulent time it has become fashionable for some Black nationalists, especially those influenced by doctrinaire Marxism, to belittle the achievements of the Black church. They thus expose their profound ignorance of African-American history.

Modern pragmatic Marxism, while historically predated by the Black church, has adopted a number of positions similar to the Black church in terms of humanitarian goals. In spite of this similarity, the myth continues that the contributions of each to the other are either nonexistent or contradictions (in the Marxist sense) that cannot be resolved. The question then arises: can Marxism and the Black church work together?

This question may be asked by those who take a simplistic view of a complex issue. Others believe that the Marxists would use the church to further their own ends and, when the dust had settled, would turn against the church. While that may have been the case in some instances, I would like to make these observations: first, in Africa Marxists aided virtually all of the former European colonies as they began their struggles for independence and self-determination. From Tanzania and Zimbabwe to Namibia, they have continued to provide this support. Second, very few of these former colonies have become satellites of Marxist nations upon attaining independence. Nonetheless, we should not lose sight of the fact that Marxists have not always done right with respect to those who have come under their influence. The present regimes of Ethiopia, Cuba, and Afghanistan have been criticized severely by people of the Third World as well as by those in the West.

Socialism from the Perspective of the Black Church

What is the significance of socialism in the African-American context? I emphasize African because the Black church was conceived in Africa and born in the United States, under the condition of slavery.

First, however, it is necessary to ask what we mean by socialism in a more general sense. This is often difficult to determine in the United States, where it is frequently dismissed as evil and atheistic. Such ignorance is to be deplored, and most likely helps to account for the lack in this country of a European-style democratic socialist party. That point of view ought also to be presented, without prejudice and as a matter of fairness. The Black church and its friends call for such a truly open democracy and its accompanying justice and liberty. At the same time, the Black church must make clear that "This is not it." While African-Americans are denied full democracy, the Third World (which includes much of the Black church) frequently has no democratic rights at all. For the Black church to refuse to acknowledge this would be to lose by default, to crucify again the Christ whose voice could not be stilled by Roman oppression.

Socialism is that philosophy which calls for a society in which the production and distribution of goods are based upon the obligation to meet the fundamental requirements of human social development and continued survival. This is a sketchy definition, but it should help us in our examination of the relationship between the Black church and Marxism and how this relationship could contribute to the new and more just society.

Fundamentally, Marxism is a reaction to capitalism, and for this reason I cannot be in agreement with it. Because it is a reaction, it tends to "compete" with, to "outvie" its stimulus rather than to exist in its own right. Let me illustrate: both capitalism and Marxism worship the same god, namely, productivity. Whether productivity is worshiped in the interest of private gain or of the common good, it is still the worship of productivity. The production manager under capitalism who fails to line the pockets of the company's shareholders will suffer; the communist manager who is unable to meet a quota in the fulfillment of the current five-year plan will be dismissed or demoted.

Another aspect of Marxism causes discomfort. In his day, Marx attacked the Social Democrats because they sought only to improve the prevailing social order while he sought to put capitalism out of business lock, stock, and barrel. It is interesting to note, therefore, that in one Marxist nation, China, the profit motive is now being encouraged—but under strict government control. That is exactly what Social Democrats have advocated: the nationalization of major industries and services while allowing minor economic activities to continue under private auspices but government control.

Marx himself, I believe, was subject to some of the shortcomings he saw in the Social Democrats. For example, according to Marx's philosophy the elimination of social classes and the "withering away" of the state would be two primary objectives, or goals, of socialism. Why are these not thought of as "take-off" points, rather than objectives? As take-off points, they would lead at once to the elimination of that narrow "patriotism" which Dr. Samuel Johnson called "the last refuge of a scoundrel." Some form of world government, and subsequent world peace, would then be a possibility. In addition, the abolition of classes could lead to the elimination of the hierarchical leadership syndrome, the occupational disease of politicians.

I have made these points against Marxism not because I am anti-Marxist but because I wish to make clear that while I advocate increased cooperation between Marxist groups and/or governments and members of the Black church, I am far from advocating the absorption of the

Black church (or the universal church) into Marxism or the other way around. While both the Black church and Marxism point toward the same goal, a new world, they want to arrive there from different starting points. Pragmatic Marxists believe that an economic revolution will generate a revolution of the human spirit; black Christians, on the other hand, hold that a spiritual revolution will generate the necessary economic revolution.

This difference in approach has been the cause of a great deal of conflict between the Black church and Marxism. This is most unfortunate, for this difference could be exploited for the benefit of all as each does what it can do best.

The Black Church and African Socialism

By upbringing and conviction, I am a Black nationalist, by self-definition, I am an African socialist. I make no apology for describing myself as a Black nationalist. I am proud of this awareness as I was and still am proud of the slogan that, unfortunately, is rarely heard today: "I'm black and I'm proud!" Only when I am proud of that which I am, African and American, will I be able to take pride in being part of that greater entity, the human race.

The fact that I am a Black nationalist does not imply that first, I relegate those blacks whose thinking does not coincide with mine to the status of "house niggers." That happened with the Black nationalists of Malcom X's time who separated blacks into the categories of "field" and "house niggers." To do this would make me guilty of that intolerance which I abhor among those who would defend and preserve the status quo. Here I echo Pogo: "We finally met the enemy face to face and, behold, the enemy was us!"

Secondly, I am not attempting to glorify or romanticize the African past. I do hold, however, that both capitalism and communism could profit from a study of African socialism, a society-oriented rather than an individual-oriented way of life. John Donne, the 17th-century cleric and poet, showed a similar orientation when, in his *Devotions,* he proclaimed, "I am involved in Mankind." Donne said this at the beginning of the European cultural upheaval, the Industrial Revolution, that has since caused the world much grief.

While many persons will be familiar with the critiques of Marxism, relatively few will know a great deal about the interpretation of African socialism. The best explication of this way of life known to me is offered by President Julius Nyerere of Tanzania, a devout Roman Catholic. In his famous essay, *African Socialism: Ujamaa in Practice,* he wrote:

> Apart from the anti-social effects of the accumulation of personal wealth, the very desire to accumulate it must be interpreted as a "vote of no-confidence" in the social system. For when a society is so organized that it cares about its individuals . . . no individual . . . should worry about what will happen to him tomorrow if he does not hoard his wealth today. Society itself should look after him, or his widow, or his orphans.
>
> This is what traditional African society succeeded in doing because he lacked personal wealth; he could depend on the wealth produced by the community . . . .
>
> We don't need Karl Marx or Adam Smith to find out that neither the land nor the hoe actually produces wealth. And we don't need to take degrees in economics to know that neither the worker nor the landlord produces land. *Land is God's gift to man.*[1]

To this President Nyerere might have added that land is God's gift to all living things.

It now becomes obvious that the early Christians (sometimes erroneously described as the "first communists"), African socialists, and Marxists have this in common: a commitment and an endeavor to ensure, as far as it is possible, the well-being of each individual in society, for without society there can be no individuals and without individuals there can be no society. I do not wish to claim that all governments professing to be either Marxist or African socialist meet or even attempt to meet these ideals. Indeed, some regimes have used these ideals to camouflage the most obscene atrocities against those whom they misrule, just as certain other governments have put the highest principles of Christianity to similar misuse. Yet it is ironic that the aspiration to ensure the well-being of each individual is less likely to be achieved in those societies which believe in and practice the cult of the individual, where each person clamors to be allowed to "do my thing." It is more likely to be achieved in "structured" or "primitive" societies where the individual is required to abdicate his or her individuality (but not personality, for this is held sacred) for the common good.

Consider these recent newspaper reports. One American in seven (34.4 million people or 15% of the population) lives below the official poverty line. That line set the annual income for a family of four at $9,862, and this works out as a daily income of $5.40 per person. If this were computed in terms of an eight-hour work day, it would come to 76.5 cents an hour (and the minimum hourly wage at this writing is $3.50). We also read that cheese distribution to the poor was cut back in July 1983 by the U.S. Department of Agriculture because of the adverse effect it was having on sales in the commercial market. How can a country, the majority of whose citizens profess to be Christian, allow people to go hungry when there is an abundance of food simply because of the demands of the profit-seekers? Whatever happened to simple compassion? In a society that encourages me to "do my thing," such antisocial behavior comes naturally.

Genuine Christians, including black Christians, call this caring for the needy an expression of the kingdom of God on earth, while Marxists would describe it as a consequence of the classless society. The projects of both movements can be dismissed as mere utopias unless we strip the term *utopia* of its negative connotations. Translated into concrete terms, *utopia* becomes an actual possibility through combined human effort. In this historical effort, often designated as *praxis*, black Christians and Marxists can come together.

Again and again we have heard the charge: "The church is being used as a tool by the Marxists." Those who voice this opinion obviously have never been victims of oppression or, if they have, have never really been aware of the fact. Oppression, as its victims know, is a situation so intolerable that the victims will employ any means available to get out from under it. Let me illustrate my point. Here is a wolf attacking an innocent lamb for its breakfast and the shepherd comes along to save the lamb. The wolf tells the lamb, "Don't go with him. He is raising you only to sell to the slaughterhouse." Now sheep may be a symbol of foolishness, but it would be an utterly stupid lamb that would choose immediate death at the fangs of the wolf to deferred death from the knife of the slaughterer.

As a Black theologian, I believe that Christians must study and work together with those who represent the "socialist vision" and do so in a conscious and critical way without trying to dissolve one into the other. Of primary importance is our commitment to the fashioning of a new world, worthy of the new human being who is beginning to appear but has not yet fully emerged. I was encouraged in this approach by the report of the speech of Archbishop Edward Scott, primate of the Anglican Church of Canada, when he exhorted the 5000 Christians attending the 1983 Conference of the World Council of Churches to "break out of their cultural captivity under capitalism or communism."

The ultimate aim of the Black church, in my view, is not the triumph of any particular system, be it capitalist or Marxist. Its sole aim is the transformation of society, with black people initially but also with all people in mind. The best expression of the point I am trying to make can be seen in Latin America and Africa. In those areas persons and groups within the church do not opt for socialist construction (or perhaps better, reconstruction) out of historical opportunism. They rather see their commitment to socialism as inspired by a greater loyalty to the God of Jesus Christ as manifested in the Bible. As James Cone asserts, "The true church always takes sides with the poor" (and he might have added that the poor often take sides with the church), and he invites black Christians to take the same side as our God. Cone continues by saying that the civil rights era hymn "God is on our side," often criticized as poor theology, is presumptuous. At the same time, he reminds us, there is the Virgin Mary, a poor and unassuming woman who praises God in these words: "He fills the indigent with good things and sends the rich away empty."[2]

In summary, let me put again the questions, as I and others have come to understand them:

- Is Black Christianity incompatible with capitalism as black people have experienced that reality in this nation?
- Is capitalism intrinsically materialistic and atheistic?
- Is it possible for true Christians to work together with capitalists?

Inverting the questions in this way, we can also affirm that the dialogue between black Christians and Marxists is open. The highway to the future has to be opened through the jungle of oppression and bigotry with the dynamite of steadfast purpose and paved with peace and justice. If that goal is shared by Christians and Marxists, if we can work together as friends and comrades, then I offer to our common venture a heartfelt Amen!

Epilogue: Christians, Marxists, and the Common Human Future

by Faith E. Burgess

The preceding pages have offered a brief description of the thought of Karl Marx, the multifaceted movement his writings have inspired, and the continuing encounter of Christians and Marxists. It is the hope of the authors that readers will be encouraged to undertake further studies in these areas. As was noted earlier, it has been our intention to unlock for Christians the previously closed bookcase containing "the many faces of Marxism."

Marx the Man and Thinker

Important as it is to know something about the life of Karl Marx, it is even more essential to grasp the uniqueness of his thought. The early chapters of this book were directed toward that goal. One cannot understand Marxism without coming to terms with his anthropology, his materialist view of history, and above all, for Christians, his critique of religion. Marx's anthropology is decisive for understanding his critique of religion. For Marx, a person is what he or she does. In a capitalist society, however, this leads to the problem of alienation, for there persons no longer have control over what they do or the products they produce. Here Marx's concept of history is introduced, for history records the inevitability of class struggles between those who exploit and those who are exploited. Only as one is able to control history, that

139

is, change it by revolutionary means, can one keep from being controlled by the forces of history. It is at this point that Marx talks about revolutionary *praxis* or activity.

What about Marx's critique of religion? The question of just how essential atheism is to his overall thought has been raised several times in this book. His atheistic stance cannot easily be ignored or dismissed. Nor is it to be accounted for as a reaction to the inability of 19th-century Christianity to respond to the desperate plight of peasants and industrial workers. No, Marx's critique of religion is tied to his basic anthropology. He really believed that human beings were capable of achieving their own salvation—understood, of course, in terms of life here and now. Marx had no interest in an existence beyond this one and he refused to speculate about an afterlife. Religion, in his opinion, was not only irrelevant but was a negative factor which prevented persons from taking charge of their own destiny. Nevertheless, while atheism was integral to Marx's thought, it did not preclude the possibility of conversations between Christians and Marxists on issues of mutual concern.

The Many Faces of Marxism

This volume has attempted to show the wide variety of expressions of Marxism throughout the world. Those wishing to dismiss Marxism without a closer look have tended toward a simplistic equation of Marxism and communism and socialism. This tendency does not contribute to genuine understanding. Political developments in Eastern Europe, for example, differ a great deal from what has occurred in the Marxist-influenced countries of Asia and Africa. Soviet-style Marxist-Leninism, moreover, stands in sharp contrast to the sophisticated critical Marxism and the democratic socialism of Western Europe.

Or consider the influence of this movement on contemporary Christian theology. Latin American liberation theology, which clearly depends upon Marxist categories and social analysis, has entered into a more extensive encounter with Marxist thought than any other theology. Yet even the recent theology of hope, widely known in Europe and the United States, owes much to Marxist questions and insights. This theology was stimulated by the thought of the philosopher Ernst Bloch, who counted himself a Marxist (albeit a somewhat unusual one). In addition, theologians other than those mentioned have reacted in positive or negative ways to Marxist thought. Both in terms of its political and its religious impact, Marxism resists reduction to a single uniform philosophy or practice.

The Christian-Marxist Dialogue

It is somewhat ironical that at a time when American Christians are moving tentatively toward conversation with Marxists that the dialogue is considered an event of the past in other parts of the world. The European enthusiasm for Christian-Marxist dialogue blossomed in the early 1960s and then withered with the world political events of the late 1960s and early 1970s. On the American scene, the strident anticommunism of the 1950s undercut the possibility of dialogue when European Christians were experiencing it. Even now, several decades later, it is most difficult for American Christians to enter the discussion. Most Europeans, however, show little more than antiquarian interest in such conversations today.

Nevertheless, the dialogue continues to be of importance. Today such an encounter is possible only if entered into fully by Christians and Marxists alike. Both parties must be convinced of the necessity to understand each other better, and both must be committed to a joint searching for truth. As we have noted earlier, the dialogue is not without its stumbling blocks. Most evident of these would be the massive differences between Christians and Marxists with respect to such concepts as God, sin, evil, grace, and redemption. Disagreement on these central concepts, however, need not end the dialogue; topics of urgent significance for the human venture await the shared reflection of Christians and Marxists.

The National Conference on Christianity and Marxism

The three-year study process in which the authors of this book participated came to its culmination in a major national conference in April 1983. Sponsored by Lutheran World Ministries, the conference met under the theme "The Challenge and the Necessity of the Christian-Marxist Encounter." All of the major presentors—Christian and Marxist—stressed the importance of ongoing contact and conversation. They agreed that the dialogue between Christians and Marxists must go on and ought to be expanded.

The first speaker at the conference was Dr. Howard Parsons, chairperson of the Department of Philosophy at the University of Bridgeport, Connecticut. A participant in the dialogue and a frequent lecturer in Eastern Europe, Dr. Parsons represented a Marxist-Leninist viewpoint and addressed the topic "Marxists and Christians: Toward Dialogue and Common Action." His lecture compared Jesus and Marx with respect to concerns shared by both. He noted that both affirmed the social dimension of personhood, called for struggle within the advancing historical process, and understood that the overcoming of human alienation in history was dependent on forces beyond human control. Parsons saw Jesus as the leader of a revolutionary movement which failed because it "did not have the requisite number, unity, and class consciousness." At the same time, "his spiritual movement succeeded insofar as the creative, redemptive love in him as his fellowship with the disciples arose in resurrected form after his death and became the guiding spirit of the early Christian community."

Stressing the need for continuing dialogue, Parsons listed what Christians can learn from Marxists and what Marxism could learn from Christianity. In the former category he noted two ways in which Marxism could help Christians understand the modern world. First, he said, "Marxism is a product of the modern industrial-urban-scientific-technological revolution. It provides a guide through the complex conditions of modern social life to a more humanized world. It is a method for understanding and changing those conditions—economic, political, social—which determine to a large degree the life and thought of individual persons." Second, Parsons identified the tool of class analysis. "The first task for believers," he pointed out, "is brotherly/sisterly love as a way of life—and this ought to include the 120 million Christians in the United States—and understanding of the class origins, the structural base, of suffering and injustice. The next task is to enter into organized political action to halt the drift toward further suffering and injustice." Turning to what Marxists could learn from Christians, Parsons listed the following: "The meaning and value of I-Thou relationships; the role of personal and interpersonal factors in history; and the hazards of power." He closed his presentation with an urgent plea: "Christians and Marxists must, among other things, seek to understand each other, enter into dialogue, and engage in communication."

A second representative of the Marxist tradition was Dr. Bogdan Denitch, professor of sociology at the Graduate School of the City University of New York and a former union organizer for the AFL-CIO. Denitch argued eloquently for democratic socialism as a political option in North America, and clearly distanced himself from major emphases of Marxist-Leninist theory and practice. He also dealt directly with many of the misperceptions Christians have about Marxism. First of those is the assumption that Marxism is monolithic.

Marxist tradition has been enormously rich in spinning off a number of schools and sub-schools and it is open to at least as many interpretations as Christianity and as little practice as Christianity. There are a great number of things that it is not. It is a hard discipline involving serious intellectual engagement. It is not a catharsis for the oppressed and the poor alone, because if it was that alone then it would be a series of inchoate rebellions. It (socialism) is an attempt to deal with the problems of modern industrial society and to give meaning to the political activity of literally millions both in advanced industrial countries and the Third World.[1]

In separating democratic socialism from what bears the name of socialism in the nations of Eastern Europe, Denitch argued that true socialism must always be democratic.

I remember those countless times when I spoke to groups of industrial workers in Canada, the United States, or in Western Europe. They would say, "Socialism? You mean that system in Eastern Europe? You mean the Soviet Union? If that is what socialism is, we do not want it!" And they were right, not wrong. We do not want less trade union rights, we do not want less democracy, we do not want less participation, we do not want less of an ability to develop than we have under capitalism. We want more! We want an expansion of democracy! That is what socialism is: the expansion of it (democracy) from the political into the social and economic spheres . . . . Socialism can be nothing if it is not democratic. Socialism can only be a system which is consciously and deliberately built by people who build that system because they want to build it— that is, it is based on vast majorities (of the people).[2]

Denitch admitted that socialists had to deal with the hard problems raised by crimes done in the name of socialism just as Christians have had to confront the consequences of crimes done in the name of Christianity. Awareness of our mutual failures should make us more cautious about hasty judgments concerning either Christianity or Marxism.

A third lecturer at this conference was a leading black theologian, Dr. James Cone, Charles A. Briggs Professor of Systematic Theology at Union Theological Seminary in New York City. Cone noted that it has only been with the emergence of Latin American liberation theology with its "affirmation of Marxist class analysis and its vehement rejection of United States capitalism (that) white and black theologians were challenged by a Marxist perspective that was not defined by Soviet Russia or its satellites." He accepted Marxist social analysis as a necessary tool for uncovering structural injustice in capitalistic societies and, indeed, in practices and pronouncements of government as well.

Because such analysis can uncover that which persons in power tend to hide, it even has usefulness in the scrutiny of the doctrine and practice of the churches. While open to the use of Marxism as an instrument of social criticism, Cone rejected its substitution for the Christian faith.

Professor Cone declared that within the context of the struggle for freedom by oppressed people both Christians and Marxists would discover common ground. As he noted, "the concern for justice is the starting point of Christian obedience. No one can be a follower of Jesus Christ without a political commitment that expresses one's solidarity with the victim." Nevertheless, despite the possibility of closer working relationships with Marxists, Cone denied that Marxism could replace Christian faith or be viewed as on a par with it. Not even the struggle for justice is the ultimate goal of faith. It is rather a "witness to God's eschatological righteousness," Cone said, and affirms a hope rooted in the cross and resurrection of Christ and which "reaches beyond the world."

The closing conference lecturer was Dr. Jan Milič Lochman, rector of the University of Basel and professor of systematic theology. Professor Lochman was a participant in the pioneer Christian-Marxist dialogue of the mid-1960s in Czechoslovakia. Speaking on the theme "Christ and/or Prometheus," he noted that the hero of Greek mythology, Prometheus, was a favorite symbol of Marx and Marxists because of his sense of solidarity with a suffering humanity, his (proletarian) enslavement, and his refusal to bow to the oppressive will of the gods. Lochman suggested that a closer look at this mythical figure would disclose the way in which he also represented "the dynamic aspect of our own radical heritage" as Christians. The entire prophetic tradition, he noted, protests against every attempt to separate God from humanity by means of a dualistic understanding of existence. Yet it was in Jesus the Christ that the historical, future-oriented, and liberating vision of God's action for humanity came to its fullest expression. Such a vision, he declared, does not lead to quietism and indifference but to active participation in a struggle for justice which expects the final liberation of God. When Christians fail to act in accord with that vision and sink into "one-dimensional" spirituality, the "Promethean people," and especially Marxists, have been justifiably alienated.

While salvation in the biblical sense is not achieved by human activity, Lochman made clear that "the biblical understanding of grace in no way excludes or depreciates human activity." Basic differences between Marxists and Christians remain, he acknowledged, but dialogue must continue, including the areas of disagreement. Dialogue, however, is not an end in itself, but is prelude to joint or common action. It is this willingness to work together that Lochman saw as a central purpose of the Christian-Marxist dialogue. Activity directed toward the attainment of greater justice—political activity—is an urgent summons to both Marxists and Christians. In summary, Lochman spoke of that common task. "That humanizing task, says the young Karl Marx, is to change all the conditions under which man is an oppressed, enslaved, destitute, and dispossessed being. This is a genuine Promethean mission. Christians and Marxists, together with all people of good will, should share it."

The Common Agenda

Lochman's recommendation stresses not only the possibility but the necessity of joint action by Christians and Marxists. His words were echoed by Professor Howard Parsons:

> The necessity for dialogue is our necessity to live and develop as persons and as a species, and hence the necessity to solve the common global problems that threaten our life and future. Such are the problems of nuclear holocaust, poverty, and injustice. The nuclear powers now have megatonnage a million times that of the Hiroshima bomb—enough to kill everyone in the world 25 times. One-half to one billion of the world's 4.5 billion people suffer from hunger or malnutrition, as well as disease and illiteracy. Hundreds of millions in Latin America, South Africa, and elsewhere live under brutal dictatorships. Injustice rooted in race, gender, age, and other conditions is widespread.[3]

Given such conditions, what might be the agenda for common activity by Christians and Marxists? The possibilities are numerous. Let me suggest at this point three major areas of mutual concern: the struggle for social justice, the search for human liberation, and the longing for a hopeful vision of the future.

The Struggle for Social Justice

Modern technological society frequently is viewed as the epitome of progress. Its dehumanizing qualities are not always recognized, and its indifference to moral values is often overlooked. There are many evidences that the administration of justice is not impartial with respect to the rich and the poor. Prisoners and death row inmates represent the indigent in disproportion to the actual perpetrators of crimes. Endemic poverty, malnutrition, disease, and illiteracy afflict the lives of greater numbers of Americans than we care to admit. Added to this are the destructive effects of pervasive racism.

The struggle for social justice in a democratic society like our own is far from over. Essentially that struggle pits powerless individuals and groups against unresponsive social systems and inhumane social attitudes. Both Christians and Marxists have a stake in working together for a society which exhibits a greater degree of economic and political justice and which seeks to create opportunity for all of its citizens.

The Search for Human Liberation

More of our contemporaries live under politically repressive regimes than in nations where they have some opportunity to influence their governments. We have too easily equated totalitarian rule with the communist states of Eastern Europe. At the same time we have refused to recognize the equally despicable capitalist dictatorships in other parts of the world and particularly in Latin America. Our government, acting in the name of national security and anticommunism, has supported many of these regimes and ignored the terrible suffering of their citizens.

Such oppression—the denial of all that we understand freedom to be—cannot be permitted to continue. To refuse to have concern for those in any form of bondage in any nation is simply not an option for Christians. Our commitment to Christ is at the same time a commitment to our neighbors. Christians should seek to make common cause with those who work to end such oppression. This is an essential item on the agenda of the Christian-Marxist dialogue.

The Longing for a Vision of Hope

Earlier in this volume we referred to the fact that many oppressed people see in Marxism a vision of hope for the future. This occurs during a period of history when much of Western civilization is experiencing cultural and moral malaise. Large numbers of persons in the Third World and elsewhere view the United States as a nation which acts out of narrow self-interest as it seeks to assure American prosperity and dominance. Such self-interest, whether exhibited by Americans or others, offers no hope to the world and little lasting comfort at home.

Christians hold to a hope which reaches beyond this world and this time, but that hope has meaning for our present existence as well. Our faith-nurtured expectation impels us to offer a vision of hope for all of our contemporaries. Karl Marx's rejection of religion was due in no small part to his perception of an unresponsive church, living in a "spiritual" world, and unconcerned about the suffering of people caught in an unjust social system. Today the Christian church must not only hear the cries of the oppressed but be in the forefront of those working to secure greater justice. In that process we have much to learn from a man who dealt with similar concerns more than a century ago. The shaping of a shared vision of hope for the world is an item of crucial importance on the agenda of the Christian-Marxist dialogue.

Christian participation in that dialogue and in common efforts for a more just and humane society are inspired and sustained by that one who was and remains God's good word for humanity. All that we do has its center in Jesus the Christ. As Nicholas Lash, a British theologian who has reflected on the relationship between Christian theology and Marxist thought, has put it:

> I confess that, in the light of our present experience of limited resources, of appalling and deepening world-wide economic misery, of particular revolutions whose dawning is swiftly eclipsed by new forms of oppression, of powerful structures of exploitative egotism self-described as oases of freedom, I see no rational grounds for optimism concerning the future of mankind. But there does exist, with whatever fragility and ambivalence, a form of hope, focused in the death of one man interpreted as resurrection, for which the struggle for humanity is deemed to be worthwhile because not just that one man's death but the entire wilderness of the world's Gethsemane is trusted to be the expression of that mystery whose truth will be all men's freedom.[4]

Notes

Chapter 1

1. Robert C. Tucker, ed. *The Marx-Engels Reader*, 2nd ed. (New York: W.W. Norton, 1972), p. 682.
2. David McLellan, *Karl Marx: His Life and Thought* (New York: Harper Colophon Books, 1973), p. 7.
3. Arend Th. van Leeuwen, *Critique of Heaven: The Gifford Lectures for 1970* (New York: Scribners, 1972), p. 40.
4. Loyd D. Easton and Kurt H. Guddat, eds., *Writings of the Young Marx on Philosophy and Society* (New York: Anchor, 1967), p. 39.
5. McLellan, p. 32.
6. Easton, p. 65.
7. Karl Marx, *Karl Marx: Early Writings*, trans. and ed. by T.B. Bottomore (New York: McGraw-Hill, 1963), p. 176.
8. Maximilien Rubel and Margaret Manale, *Marx Without Myth* (New York: Harper & Row, 1975), pp. 42-43.
9. Tucker, p. 133.
10. McLellan, p. 154.
11. Ibid., p. 452.
12. Ibid., p. 177.
13. Ibid., p. 230.
14. Rubel, p. 100.
15. Boris Nicolaievsky and Otto Maenchen-Helfen, *Karl Marx: Man and Fighter* (Middlesex, England: Penguin Books, 1976), p. 261.
16. McLellan, p. 235.
17. Rubel, p. 148.

18. Ibid., p. 153.
19. Ibid., p. 169.
20. Ibid., p. 178.
21. Tucker, p. 518.
22. McLellan, p. 455.
23. Ibid., pp. 455-456.
24. Tucker, p. 625.
25. Rubel, p. 278.
26. Ibid., p. 294.
27. Nicolaievsky, p. 260.
28. Rubel, p. 298.
29. Tucker, p. 675.
30. McLellan, p. 456.
31. Ibid., pp. 447-448.
32. Rubel, p. 329.
33. Tucker, p. 682.

Chapter 2

1. Karl Marx, *Theses on Feuerbach,* in *The Marx-Engels Reader,* 2nd ed., ed. Robert C. Tucker (New York: Norton, 1978), p. 145.
2. Ibid., p. 143.
3. Marx, *Economic and Philosophical Manuscripts of 1844,* in *Reader,* p. 72.
4. Ibid., p. 76.
5. Ibid., p. 70.
6. Ibid., p. 72.
7. Ibid., p. 64.
8. Ibid., pp. 84-85.

Chapter 3

1. Karl Marx, *Contribution to the Critique of Hegel's Philosophy,* in *The Marx-Engels Reader,* 2nd ed., ed. Robert C. Tucker (New York: Norton, 1978), pp. 53-54.
2. Marx, *Economic and Philosophical Manuscripts of 1844,* in *Reader,* p. 92.

Chapter 4

1. Karl Marx, *Karl Marx: Early Writings,* trans. and ed. by T.B. Bottomore (New York: McGraw-Hill, 1963), p. 166.
2. Karl Marx, *Theses on Feuerbach,* in *The Marx-Engels Reader,* 2nd ed., ed. Robert C. Tucker (New York: Norton, 1978), p. 145.
3. Marx, *The German Ideology: Part 1,* in *Reader,* pp. 155-56.
4. Ibid., p. 157.

5. Marx, *Manifesto of the Communist Party*, in *Reader*, p. 473.
6. Marx, *Preface to A Contribution to the Critique of Political Economy*, in *Reader*, pp. 4-5.
7. Marx, *Grundrisse*, in *Reader*, p. 241.
8. Ibid., p. 233.
9. Marx, *The German Ideology: Part 1*, in *Reader*, p. 169.
10. Marx, *Grundrisse*, in *Reader*, p. 243.
11. Marx, *The German Ideology: Part 1*, in *Reader*, p. 186.
12. Marx, *Manifesto of the Communist Party*, in *Reader*, p. 475.
13. Ibid., p. 483.
14. Marx, *The German Ideology: Part 1*, in *Reader*, p. 191.
15. Marx, *Preface to A Contribution to the Critique of Political Economy*, in *Reader*, p. 5.
16. Marx, *Grundrisse, in Reader*, p. 233.
17. Marx, *The Eighteenth Brumaire of Louis Bonaparte*, in *Reader*, p. 595.
18. Marx, *The German Ideology: Part 1*, in *Reader*, p. 158.
19. Marx, *Economic and Philosophical Manuscripts*, in *Reader*, p. 92.
20. Marx, *The German Ideology: Part 1*, in *Reader*, p. 155.
21. Ibid., p. 164.
22. Ibid., pp. 172-73.
23. Marx, *Contribution to the Critique of Hegel's Philosophy of Right: Introduction*, in *Reader*, pp. 53-54.
24. Marx, *Manifesto of the Communist Party*, in *Reader*, p. 477.
25. Marx, *Contribution to the Critique of Hegel's Philosophy of Right: Introduction*, in *Reader*, p. 64.
26. Marx, *The German Ideology: Part 1*, in *Reader*, pp. 192-93.
27. Marx, *Preface to a Contribution to the Critique of Political Economy*, in *Reader*, p. 5.
28. Marx, *The German Ideology: Part 1*, in *Reader*, pp. 192-93.
29. Ibid., p. 169.
30. Marx, *Manifesto of the Communist Party*, in *Reader*, p. 484.
31. Marx, *The German Ideology, Part 1*, in *Reader*, pp. 191-92.
32. Marx, *Economic and Philosophical Manuscripts*, in *Reader*, p. 80.
33. Marx, *The German Ideology: Part 1*, in *Reader*, p. 160.
34. Ibid., p. 193.
35. Marx, *Manifesto of the Communist Party*, in *Reader*, p. 491.
36. Ibid., p. 490.
37. David McLellan, *The Alleged Splits in the International*, from *The Thought of Karl Marx: An Introduction* (New York: Harper and Row, 1971), p. 184.
38. Marx, *Critique of the Gotha Program*, in *Reader*, p. 538.
39. Marx, *Capital*, vol. 3, in *Reader*, p. 441.
40. Marx, *Preface to a Contribution to the Critique of Political Economy*, in *Reader*, p. 5.

41. Marx, *Contribution to the Critique of Hegel's Philosophy of Right: Introduction,* in *Reader,* p. 60.

Chapter 5

1. Massimo Salvadori, ed., *Modern Socialism* (New York: Harper and Row, 1968), p. 4. Much of the material in this chapter is taken from this source.
2. The early 19th century was characterized by socialists such as Robert Owen, Claude-Henri de Saint-Simon, Charles Fourier, Louis Auguste Blanqui, Pierre Joseph Proudhon, Ferdinand LaSalle, Moses Hess, and Mikhail Bakunin. It was an age of utopian socialist experiments such as New Lanark, New Harmony, the North American Phalanx, Icarian Colonies and many others in Western Europe and the United States. Great Britain and France were the intellectual and political cradles of socialism. Political action began with semiclandestine societies in France, stimulated by the freer atmosphere created in the Revolution of 1830; it had its baptism of fire in Paris in June 1848, and ended in the bloodbath of the Paris Commune in 1871.
3. In its technical sense, communism refers to that final stage of history when all conflicts have been resolved, all class strife ended, and humanity can live in total harmony and prosperity. Even for Marxists such a utopian state remains a distant dream. In the political sense, however, the term "communism" refers to the particular form of Marxist socialism espoused by Lenin and practiced, with varying degrees of conformity, by the Soviet Union and its closest allies. It is not always easy to distinguish between "communist" and "Marxist," as in the case of Cuba or Ethiopia. Here we use the term to refer primarily to the countries of Eastern Europe.
4. A more detailed exposition of Christian-Marxist relations is found in Chapter 7.
5. The material which follows is taken largely from Paul Mojzes, *Christian-Marxist Dialogue in Eastern Europe* (Minneapolis: Augsburg, 1981), pp. 35-167.
6. Hans-Jurgen Benedict, "The Encounter of the Church and Marxism in Western Germany," in *The Encounter of the Church with Movements of Social Change in Various Cultural Contexts* (Geneva: Lutheran World Federation, Department of Studies), 1977.
7. Francis J. Murphy, "Milestones of Christian-Marxist Dialogue in France," from *Varieties of Christian-Marxist Dialogue* (Philadelphia: The Ecumenical Press, 1978), p. 146.
8. Ibid.
9. Alberto Saggese, "Christians and Marxists: The Situation in Italy," in *The Encounter of the Church with Movements of Social Change in Various Cultural Contexts:* Part 2, p. 88.

10. Cf. "The Demise of Eurocommunism," in *Newsweek,* April 21, 1980, p. 58.
11. Ibid.
12. Martti Lindqvist, "The Christian-Marxist Encounter in Finland," in *The Encounter of the Church with Movements of Social Change in Various Cultural Contexts:* Part 2, pp. 51-58.
13. Salvadori, pp. 18, 32, 36-37.

Chapter 7

1. Billy James Hargis, *Communism the Total Lie!* (Tulsa: Christian Crusade, 1963), p. 7.
2. Reinhold Niebuhr, *An Interpretation of Christian Ethics* (New York: Seabury Press, 1979), p. 113.
3. See Dennis P. McCann, *Christian Realism and Liberation Theology* (Maryknoll, New York: Orbis Books, 1981) for a discussion of Niebuhr's position and its relation to the more recent development of liberation theology
4. See Tillich's essay, "Christianity and Marxism," reprinted in his *Political Expectations* (New York: Harper & Row, 1971), pp. 89-96.
5. Paul Oestreicher, ed., *The Christian Marxist Dialogue* (New York: Macmillan, 1969), p. 10.
6. Jan Milič Lochman, *Encountering Marx* (Philadelphia: Fortress Press, 1977), p. 24.
7. Roger Garaudy, *From Anathema to Dialogue* (New York: Herder and Herder, 1966), p. 86.

Chapter 8

1. Walter H. Capps, *Time Invades the Cathedral* (Philadelphia: Fortress Press, 1972), pp. 25 and 34.
2. Ernst Bloch, *On Karl Marx,* trans. by John Maxwell (New York: Herder and Herder, 1971), p. 36, emphasis added.
3. Ibid., p. 23.
4. Ibid., p. 21.
5. Ernst Bloch, *Man on His Own,* trans. by E.B. Ashton (New York: Herder and Herder, 1970), p. 37.
6. Ibid., p. 39.
7. Ernst Bloch, *Atheism in Christianity,* trans. by J.T. Swann (New York: Herder and Herder, 1972), p. 264.
8. Ernst Bloch, *A Philosophy of the Future,* trans. by John Cunning (New York: Herder and Herder, 1970), p. 139.
9. Bloch, *Man on His Own,* p. 80.
10. Bloch, *On Karl Marx,* pp. 99-105.
11. Bloch, *Man on His Own,* p. 116.
12. Ibid., p. 123.

13. Ibid., p. 124.
14. Bloch, *Atheism in Christianity*, p. 239.
15. Capps, p. 150.
16. Carl Braaten and Robert Jenson, *The Futurist Option* (New York: Newman Press, 1970), p. 72.
17. Jürgen Moltmann, *The Experiment Hope*, ed. and trans. by Douglas Meeks (Philadelphia: Fortress, 1975), pp. 46-47.
18. Wolfhart Pennenberg, "The God of Hope," from *Basic Questions in Theology*, vol. II, trans. by George H. Kehm (Philadelphia: Fortress, 1971), pp. 237-39.
19. Ibid., p. 239.
20. Jürgen Moltmann, *Religion, Revolution, and the Future*, trans. by M. Douglas Meeks (New York: Scribner's, 1969), pp. 163-64.
21. See "Karl Marx, Death and the Apocalypse" in *Man on His Own*, pp. 31-72.
22. Johannes B. Metz, *Theology of the World*, trans. by William Glen-Doepel (New York: Herder and Herder, 1969), p. 110.
23. Ibid.
24. Ibid., pp. 22-23.
25. Ibid., pp. 152-53.
26. Wolfhart Pannenberg, *Theology and the Kingdom of God* (Philadelphia: Westminster, 1969), pp. 110-12.
27. Moltmann, *The Experiment Hope*, pp. 101-18.
28. Ibid., p. 39.

Chapter 9

1. José Miguez Bonino, *Doing Theology in a Revolutionary Situation* (Grand Rapids: Eerdmans, 1976), p. 93.
2. Gustavo Gutiérrez, *A Theology of Liberation* (Maryknoll, NY: Orbis, 1973), p. 167.
3. Bonino, p. 19.

Chapter 10

1. Julius K. Nyerere. *Freedom and Unity/Uhuru na Umoja:* Essays on Ujamaa—Basis of African Socialism (Dar es Salaam, Tanzania: Oxford University Press), p. 164.
2. These remarks were part of a presentation by Dr. Cone. In a recent conversation with me, he verified that he had made these assertions.

Epilogue

1. Quotations attributed to Drs. Howard Parsons, Bogdan Denitch, James Cone, and Jan Milič Lochman are from videotapes and manuscripts prepared for the National Conference on Christianity and Marxism.

These materials are held by Lutheran World Ministries, New York City.
2. Ibid.
3. Ibid.
4. Nicholas Lash, *A Matter of Hope: A Theologian's Reflections on the Thought of Karl Marx* (University of Notre Dame Press, 1982), p. 280.

Select Bibliography

The following books are recommended as guides to various aspects of Marxist thought and practice, Christian critiques of Marxism, or contributions to the continuing encounter between Christians and Marxists.

Ernst Bloch. *Atheism in Christianity: The Religion of the Exodus and the Kingdom*. Translated by J.T. Swann. Herder and Herder, 1972.

Bloch, a leading Marxist philosopher, offers a provocative reading of the Bible. His conclusion: "When Christians are really concerned with the emancipation of those who labor and are heavy-laden, and when Marxists retain the depths of the Kingdom of Freedom as the real content of revolutionary consciousness on the road to becoming true substance, the alliance between revolution and Christianity founded in the Peasant Wars may live again—this time with success" (page 272).

José Miguez Bonino. *Christians and Marxists: The Mutual Challenge to Revolution*. Hodder and Stoughton, 1976.

An Argentinian Methodist theologian and ecumenical leader, Bonino argues that Latin American Christians, seeking to make their faith historically relevant, have discovered the "unsubstitutable relevance of Marxism." Acknowledging the difference between Christianity and Marxism, he attempts to define the limits of Christian participation in a revolutionary process.

Gerd Decke, ed. *The Encounter of the Church with Movements of Social Change in Various Cultural Contexts: With Special Reference to Marxism*. Lutheran World Federation: Department of Studies, 1977.

This volume consists of papers from two LWF-sponsored conferences held in 1975 and 1976. These forums sought to describe the various encounters of the church with Marxism and to evaluate the implications of those encounters for the theology, life, and witness of the Lutheran churches.

Gustavo Gutiérrez. *A Theology of Liberation: History, Politics and Salvation.* Trans. and ed. by Sister Caridad Inda and John Eagleson. Orbis Books, 1973.

The earliest and classic statement of a "new way of doing theology" in Latin America. Gutiérrez, a Peruvian Catholic theologian, defines theology as "critical reflection on historical praxis" from the perspective of oppressed peoples. He sees theology "in direct and fruitful confrontation with Marxism," and asserts that "it is to a large extent due to Marxism's influence that theological thought, searching for its own sources, has begun to reflect on the meaning of the transformation of this world and the action of man in history" (p. 9).

Peter Hebblethwaite. *The Christian-Marxist Dialogue: Beginnings, Present Status, and Beyond.* Paulist Press, 1977.

This British Catholic theologian and journalist provides a careful record and sober assessment of modern encounters of Christians and Marxists. Because of Marxism's tendency to see itself as a "*total* ideology" (which includes atheism), Hebblethwaite concludes that "there is as yet no satisfactory synthesis between Christianity and Marxism."

Robert L. Heilbroner. *Marxism: For and Against.* W.W. Norton, 1980.

The distinguished American political economist sets forth a lucid analysis of the dynamic of Marxist thought and a penetrating critique of its contemporary usefulness. Recognizing its significant contributions, Heilbroner closes with a penetrating observation: "What remains open to question is whether Marxism itself will survive in a socialism of a truly revolutionary kind. The answer, it seems to me, hinges on whether Marxism is ultimately to be an ideology or a critical philosophy" (p. 172).

Nicholas Lash. *A Matter of Hope: A Theologian's Reflections on the Thought of Karl Marx.* University of Notre Dame Press, 1982.

Lash, a British Catholic theologian, reflects on major themes in the thought of Marx. Those themes are brought into direct relationship with Christian beliefs without sacrificing the integrity of either Marxist or Christian convictions. Throughout Lash maintains the Christological focus of human hope: "To be a Christian is to seek to conform the practice and substance of one's hope to the hope of Jesus" (p. 279).

Jan Milič Lochman. *Encountering Marx: Bonds and Barriers Between Christians and Marxists.* Fortress, 1977.

Lochman, a Czech theologian now teaching in Basel, Switzerland, partici-pated in the Christian-Marxist dialogue in Europe. This small volume is an introduction to some of Marx's leading ideas and an appreciative, though critical, Christian response. Lochman's evangelical convictions and social sensitivity contribute to the usefulness of this book.

Arthur F. McGovern. *Marxism: An American Christian Perspective.* Orbis Books, 1980.

McGovern is a Jesuit theologian teaching at the University of Detroit. He has included in a single volume a survey of Marxist thought, an account of the development of Catholic attitudes with respect to Marxism, a critique of capitalism, liberation theology, and socialism in Latin America, discussions of atheism and other topics, and reflections on Marxism in the United States. Comprehensive and fair, this book argues for Christian participation in a democratic process which takes seriously Marxist concerns as it seeks a more just, free, and egalitarian society.

David McLellan. *Karl Marx: His Life and Thought.* Harper Colophon Books, 1973.

McLellan is a leading British scholar in the area of Marxist studies. His biography of Karl Marx is sympathetic yet objective, comprehensive without being pedantic. The events of Marx's personal life are depicted in close relationship with the intellectual and political activities for which he is known. A prior reading of this biography will help situate the writings of Marx in their historical contexts.

David McLellan. *The Thought of Karl Marx: An Introduction.* Harper Torch-books, 1971.

McLellan here provides a helpful introduction to the writings of Karl Marx. The first half of the book is arranged chronologically: brief descriptions of what Marx wrote are related to the events of his life. The second half arranges excerpts from Marx's writings under the headings of alienation, historical materialism, labor, class, the party, the state, revolution, and the future com-munist society.

Paul Mojzes. *Christian-Marxist Dialogue in Eastern Europe.* Augsburg, 1981.

Mojzes, a United Methodist theologian teaching at Rosemont College in Pennsylvania, is a leading American expert on Christian-Marxist relations. His description of those relations in the socialist bloc countries of Eastern Europe is detailed, objective, and modestly hopeful. Major issues in the current Christian-Marxist dialogue are clearly identified.

Julius K. Nyerere. *Nyerere on Socialism.* Dar es Salaam: Oxford University Press, 1969.

Nyerere led the East African nation of Tanzania to independence and continues to serve as its president. This collection of essays depicts his conviction that a nondoctrinaire socialism is compatible with an enlightened, nontribal, African nationalism. A devout Catholic, Nyerere denies that African socialism is anti-Christian. His thought is particularly influential in the new African nations which have large numbers of Christians.

Paul Tillich. *The Socialist Decision.* Translated by Franklin Sherman. Harper and Row, 1977.

Tillich, a leading Lutheran theologian of this century, wrote this book between the two world wars. His views concerning religious socialism were offered as an alternative to the conservative politics of most German Christians during this period. Tillich attempted to view socialism from a theological perspective, and this book has stimulated similar efforts by other Christians.

Robert C. Tucker, ed. *The Marx-Engels Reader,* 2nd ed. W.W. Norton, 1978.

This anthology of the most significant writings of Marx and Engels offers what is needed "to acquire a thorough grounding in Marxist thought . . . introductory notes to each selection, a chronology of the careers of the two men, and a concluding bibliographic guide to some of the literature about them and their thought." Tucker is professor of politics at Princeton University.

Cornel West. *Prophesy Deliverance! An Afro-American Revolutionary Christianity.* Westminster Press, 1982.

West is professor of the philosophy of religion at Union Theological Seminary, New York City. Drawing upon the experiences of black Christians in North America, he argues for an alliance of prophetic Christianity and progressive (not Marxist-Leninist) Marxism. Radical and Christian, West seeks to contribute to the liberation of Americans from both economic oppression and racism.

The following periodicals are recommended for those who would like to pursue details of Christian-Marxist dialogue:

Occasional Papers on Religion in Eastern Europe. Published by Christians Associated for Relations with Eastern Europe. Edited by Dr. Paul Mojzes, Rosemont College, Rosemont, Pennsylvania 19010.

Religion in Eastern Europe. Published by Keston College, Heathfield Road, Keston, Kent BR26BA, England. Edited by Michael Bourdeaux.